Savoring the Seasons
with OUR BEST BITES

Tres Leches Cupcakes, see p

Savoring the Seasons

with **OUR BEST BITES**

More Than 100 Year-Round Recipes to Enjoy with Family and Friends

Sara Wells & Kate Jones

SHADOW MOUNTAIN

To my family: Eric, Tyler, Owen, and Jack. Each season of my life is sweeter with you boys in it. —Sara

To the memory of my mom, Margaret Bishop Randle, and the amazing holiday celebrations she created. —Kate

All food styling and food photography by Sara Wells, except page 161, which is by Kate Jones
Art direction by Richard Erickson
Book and cover design by Sheryl Dickert Smith
Typography by Rachael Ward
Back cover and author photos of Sara by Rebecca Smith; author photo of Kate by Sam Jones; back cover photo of Kate by Lydia McDaniel Hutson; author photo on page 1 by Jenny Flake.

Visit us at ShadowMountain.com

Library of Congress Cataloging-in-Publication Data
Wells, Sara (Sara Smith), author.
  Savoring the seasons with Our best bites / Sara Wells and Kate Jones.
     pages cm
  Summary: Cookbook based on the Our best bites blog.
  Includes index.
  ISBN 978-1-60907-132-5 (hardbound : alk. paper) 1. Seasonal cooking. I. Jones, Kate (Kate Randle), author. II. Title.
TX714.W345 2012
641.5'64—dc23
                                                                                                      2012016922

Printed in China
Regent Publishing Services Limited, Shau Kei Wan, Hong Kong
10 9 8 7 6 5 4 3 2 1

Contents

❄ WINTER

Acknowledgments

We'd like to thank our friends at Shadow Mountain who have been so patient and supportive of our ideas for this book—every single person we have worked with directly (and those who have been more behind the scenes) has done everything possible to help us realize and exceed our very best vision for this book. A million thanks to those who faithfully read *Our Best Bites*; without you, none of this would be possible. Thank you to our friends and family, both near and far—you have helped shape and support who we are and what we do every day. And finally, we are completely indebted to our husbands, Sam Jones and Eric Wells, as well as our kids Clark, Meredith, Tyler, Owen, Jack, and the yet-to-be-named Jones baby, for being endlessly patient, supportive, and loving.

Introduction

Avid readers of our blog *Our Best Bites* know that while we enjoy posting every-day recipes for busy families, we really love holidays. We love the crafts and recipes passed down from generation to generation and the memories that come along with those traditions.

When we were discussing possibilities for another cookbook, a book centered on the seasons was a very natural next step for us. From the springy smell of Brussels sprouts to grilled recipes that are perfect for a summer barbecue to cinnamon-spiced desserts in autumn to cozy soups and stews for winter, we wanted these recipes to evoke feelings and memories of each season, to inspire you to cook no matter the time of year and to create memories all year long with the people you love the most.

We hope that you'll want to cook your way through this book and as you do, you'll find recipes that will become part of your family and seasonal traditions for years to come!

Love,

Sara & Kate

Berry-Kiwi Salad with Mint-Lime Dressing, see page 21

Spring

ST. PATRICK'S DAY

Easter

- planning and planting a garden
- daffodils, tulips, and lilies in bloom
- stained fingers and the smell of vinegar from dyeing Easter eggs
- riding a bike for the first time of the year
- birds chirping in the early morning
- the sweet smell of blossoming trees
- flying kites in breezy weather
- the sight and scent of grass poking through the thawing earth

MOTHER'S DAY

IN SEASON

Artichokes, asparagus, broccoli, green beans, honeydew melons, lettuce, limes, mangoes, snow peas, spinach, strawberries, sugar snap peas

❀ SPRING

Banana Slush Punch

Kate's Grandma Randle made this punch for every family gathering, from Christmas dinner to the Fourth of July, from baby blessings to wedding showers to backyard kindergarten parties. It's not just a nostalgic favorite, it's pretty darn delicious, too.

6 cups water, divided

4 very ripe bananas

1½ cups sugar

6 cups pineapple juice (48 ounces)

2 (12-ounce) cans orange juice concentrate

1 (12-ounce) can lemonade concentrate (pink or yellow)

3 liters ginger ale or lemon-lime soda, such as Sprite

Frozen berries of choice, optional, for garnish

1. Combine 3 cups water, bananas, and sugar in a blender. Process until smooth and set aside.

2. Combine remaining water, pineapple juice, orange juice concentrate, and lemonade concentrate in a large bowl or pan, and mix well or blend with an immersion blender. Add banana mixture.

3. Divide mixture evenly among 3 freezer-safe containers or gallon-sized zip-top bags and freeze for several hours or preferably overnight. When ready to serve, place 1 container of punch mixture at a time into a punch bowl and pour 1 liter of chilled ginger ale or Sprite over it. Mix with a spoon (or immersion blender) and serve immediately. If desired, garnish with frozen berries.

Orange Rolls

In this recipe, we use the light, airy dough from our favorite Everyday Cinnamon Rolls and fill it with sweet, citrusy orange filling and then drizzle the warm rolls with a sweet orange glaze. These are perfect for breakfast on Easter morning!

Dough

1 cup milk

4 tablespoons butter, cut into chunks

3¼–3½ cups all-purpose flour, divided

1 (0.25-ounce) package instant or rapid rise yeast (about 2¼ teaspoons)

¼ cup sugar

½ teaspoon salt

1 egg

Filling

½ cup butter, softened

½ cup sugar

2 tablespoons orange zest

Glaze

¼ cup butter

1 cup powdered sugar

Enough orange juice to reach desired consistency

1. **For the dough:** Place milk and butter in a microwave-safe bowl. Heat 1 minute 30 seconds on high. Butter should be at least partially melted. Stir and set aside.

2. Whisk together 2 cups flour, yeast, sugar, and salt in a large mixing bowl. When milk mixture has cooled to warm (not hot; about 105–110 degrees F.), add it to the flour mixture along with the egg. Beat until well combined, using the paddle attachment—about 1 minute.

3. Switch to the dough hook. Add the remaining flour only until dough barely leaves the sides of the bowl. It should be very soft and slightly sticky. Continue to knead dough with mixer for 5 minutes or turn dough onto floured surface and knead for 5 minutes by hand. Allow to rest about 10 minutes while you make the filling.

4. **For the filling:** Combine ingredients in a small bowl.

5. **To assemble:** Roll dough into a rectangle about 12 x 14 inches. Spread filling mixture over the surface and use your fingers or the back of a spoon to gently spread around. Roll up from the longer side of the rectangle and pinch edges closed. Use a piece of dental floss to score the roll into 12 equal pieces and then slip the floss under the "log" and cinch off each

piece with the floss to cut into rolls. Place in a 9 x 13-inch pan that has been sprayed with nonstick cooking spray. Cover pan with a clean towel and let rise in a warm place about 30 minutes or until visibly increased in size. In the meantime, preheat oven to 350 degrees F.

6. When rolls have finished rising, bake 15–20 minutes or until light golden brown.

7. **For the glaze:** Melt butter in a small saucepan or in microwave. Add the powdered sugar and enough orange juice to reach a smooth pouring consistency. Drizzle over warm rolls.

⊕ **Quick and Easy**

ROLLOVER
Buttermilk

TIP: Don't defrost frozen blueberries before using them. Keeping the berries frozen will keep them moist and will prevent your batter from turning purple.

Blueberry Muffins

Everyone needs a great, basic blueberry muffin recipe, and this is ours! The citrus zest adds a lot of flavor to the muffins without being overwhelming, and the streusel topping is the proverbial icing on these little cakes.

1¾ cups plus 1 tablespoon all-purpose flour, divided

2¾ teaspoons baking powder

¾ teaspoon salt

½ cup plus 1 tablespoon sugar, divided

2 teaspoons orange or lemon zest

1 large egg

¾ cup buttermilk

⅓ cup canola oil

1 cup fresh or frozen blueberries

Streusel Topping

¼ cup sugar

2½ tablespoons flour

½ teaspoon cinnamon

1½ tablespoons butter

1. Preheat oven to 400 degrees F. Line a 12-cup muffin tin with cupcake liners and set aside.

2. Lightly spoon 1¾ cups flour into measuring cups and level with a knife. Combine flour with baking powder, salt, ½ cup sugar, and citrus zest in a large bowl. Make a well in the center of the mixture. Whisk together the egg, buttermilk, and oil in a separate small bowl. Add to dry ingredients, stirring just until moistened.

3. Combine remaining 1 cup flour and 1 tablespoon sugar in a small bowl and then toss blueberries into this mixture until they are well coated. Gently fold blueberry mixture into the batter. Spoon batter into lined muffin tins, filling ⅔ full.

4. **For the streusel topping:** Combine sugar, flour, and cinnamon. Cut in butter with a pastry cutter or two butter knives until the mixture is crumbly. Sprinkle over batter and bake 18 minutes or until tops are golden and a toothpick inserted into the center of a muffin comes out clean. Remove from oven and allow to cool in the pan for 5 minutes. Transfer to a cooling rack.

♥ **Family Favorite**
❄ **Freezer Meal**
☆ **Make Ahead**

MAKE-AHEAD AND FREEZER INSTRUCTIONS:

Disregard egg-wash step. After pastry-wrapped sausages are cut into pieces, place in a single layer and flash freeze until dough is no longer sticky to the touch. Place in a freezer-safe container, or zip-top bag and store in freezer up to 1 month. Alternately, they can be stored in the refrigerator up to 2 days before baking. The baking instructions remain the same whether the sausages are refrigerated or frozen.

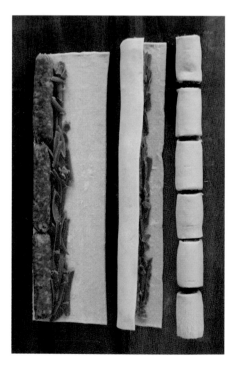

Pastry-Wrapped Breakfast Sausages with Maple-Dijon Dipping Sauce

These pigs-in-a-blanket with a sophisticated twist are a hit with kids and adults!

1 sheet frozen puff pastry, thawed in refrigerator

1 (12-ounce) package breakfast sausage links (about 14 small links)

½ cup shredded cheese of your choice, optional

1 egg, lightly beaten with 2 teaspoons water, for egg wash

1. Gently unfold the puff pastry sheet onto a lightly floured surface. Lightly sprinkle the surface of the dough with flour and roll into a 12 x 12-inch square. Use a pizza cutter or sharp knife to slice into 4 equal strips.

2. Working with one strip of dough at a time, place 3 sausages lengthwise down one side of the dough strip. If extra space remains, trim another sausage to fit so entire length of dough strip is covered. If using cheese, sprinkle about 2 tablespoons shredded cheese next to the sausages. Starting from the edge where the sausages are, gently roll dough so it wraps around the sausage and cheese and folds over onto itself. Gently press or pinch dough to seal and softly roll to smooth out surface. Repeat with remaining puff pastry strips, sausages, and cheese.

3. Using a pastry brush, brush tops of rolls with egg wash. Using a sharp knife, slice rolls into 1½ to 2-inch pieces. Place on a parchment-lined baking sheet and bake 15–20 minutes or until light golden brown. Cool 3–5 minutes and serve with Maple-Dijon Dipping Sauce or pure maple syrup for dipping.

Maple-Dijon Dipping Sauce

2 tablespoons Dijon mustard

4 tablespoons pure maple syrup

4 tablespoons mayonnaise

Whisk ingredients together until combined.

ROLLOVERS
Feta cheese
Green onions
Sour cream

Mediterranean Egg Scramble

These wraps are a quick and delicious way to start off your morning! If you have extra time, make homemade crêpes to wrap them in; otherwise, you can use store-bought crêpes cooked at home or warm flour tortillas.

6 eggs

¼ cup sour cream

¼ teaspoon kosher salt

2–3 cracks freshly ground black pepper

½ teaspoon dried basil

½ teaspoon dried oregano

¼ teaspoon garlic powder

¾ cup crumbled feta cheese, plus more
   for topping

1 teaspoon butter

2 tablespoons diced roasted red peppers

2 tablespoons minced green onions

Crêpes or warm flour tortillas

1. Preheat a skillet over medium heat.

2. Whisk the eggs, sour cream, salt, pepper, basil, oregano, and garlic powder together. Gently add the crumbled feta cheese. When the skillet is hot, add 1 teaspoon butter and then add the egg mixture and allow it to begin to set up. Scrape the bottom of the skillet to allow the liquid parts to cook. Stir in the roasted red peppers and green onions. Cook eggs until the desired doneness is reached. Serve immediately.

3. Before wrapping the scrambled eggs in crêpes or warm flour tortillas, sprinkle the mixture with a little extra feta cheese, if desired.

Spinach-Artichoke Quiche

Other than an extra hour of undisturbed sleep, nothing says "I love you, Mom!" like breakfast in bed. Whip up this quiche the night before and then serve it with freshly squeezed orange juice and a jelly jar filled with hand-picked flowers from the yard.

Serves 8

☆ **Make Ahead**

ROLLOVER
Parmesan cheese

1 (9-inch) unbaked pie crust, either store-bought or homemade

1 (9-ounce) box frozen spinach, thawed

8 ounces bacon, cooked and crumbled, divided

¼ cup chopped marinated artichoke hearts

2 cups grated Gruyère cheese

½ cup freshly grated Parmesan cheese

3 large eggs

1½ cups half-and-half

2 tablespoons finely chopped onion

1 tablespoon Dijon mustard

¾ teaspoon kosher salt

½ teaspoon freshly cracked black pepper

½ tablespoon fresh thyme leaves, or ½ teaspoon dried thyme

1. Preheat oven to 350 degrees F. Place pie crust dough in a 9-inch pie, quiche, or tart pan. If using a pie plate, flute the edges. If using a quiche or tart pan, trim excess dough from edge with a knife. Place a layer of foil over the pie dough, extending over the edges of the pan. Place pie weights or dry beans on top of foil. Bake 15 minutes. Remove weights and foil and use a fork to prick the dough several times. Return to oven and bake 5–10 minutes longer, until set and light golden brown. Remove crust from oven.

2. Squeeze liquid from spinach. Use a clean cloth or paper towel to absorb all excess moisture. Chop spinach and then spread it out on the bottom of the pie crust. Reserve 2 tablespoons bacon. Sprinkle remaining bacon and artichoke hearts evenly over the spinach. Top with the grated cheeses.

3. Combine eggs, half-and-half, onion, mustard, salt, pepper, and thyme in a medium-sized mixing bowl. Whisk until well combined and then pour into pie crust. Sprinkle reserved bacon on top. Bake 30–40 minutes at 350 degrees F. until set in the middle and light golden brown. Cool at least 15 minutes before slicing. This can be served warm, at room temperature, or cold.

Author's Note

I love a classic "Dutch Baby,"
cooked in a hot cast-iron skillet,
but I sometimes find them hard
to serve, especially for my little
kids. I came up with this recipe
so their little fingers could just
dip and munch, and the treat
has been a family favorite ever
since! —*Sara*

Mini Puffed Oven Pancakes with Easy Berry Sauce

These bite-sized puffs take just seconds to whip up and are even more fun to eat than they are to look at! Try them with the Easy Berry Sauce for a fun weekend breakfast or brunch, or let little ones dip them in bowls of maple syrup instead.

½ cup flour

¾ cup milk

2 large eggs

⅛ teaspoon salt

2–3 tablespoons butter, melted

Powdered sugar

Whipped cream or nondairy whipped topping, optional

1. Place a nonstick mini muffin pan in the oven and heat to 400 degrees F. While oven is heating, place flour, milk, eggs, and salt in a blender and blend until smooth. Carefully remove the pan from the oven (don't forget it's hot!) and quickly spray the wells with nonstick spray. Fill muffin wells three-fourths full with batter.

2. Bake 12–18 minutes, until batter is puffed and slightly golden on top. Remove puffs and place on plate or platter. Drizzle with melted butter and sprinkle with powdered sugar. Drizzle with Easy Berry Sauce and top with whipped cream, or serve with sauce and/or maple syrup for dipping. Serve immediately.

Easy Berry Sauce

6 large frozen or fresh strawberries

3 tablespoons berry jam

Sugar, to taste

If using frozen berries, place berries and jam in a microwave-safe bowl and heat for about 1 minute. Use a fork to stir and mash everything together (cut strawberries if necessary), or place everything in a blender and pulse a few times until desired consistency is reached. Add sugar to taste for sweetness and a few teaspoons of water or juice only if needed for consistency.

Strawberry Croissant French Toast

Croissants are perfect in this baked French toast because after soaking up the creamy lemon mixture, they puff up light and crispy. We love this recipe in the spring when you can get large flats of gorgeous strawberries at a great price.

6 large butter croissants

1 (8-ounce) package cream cheese

Zest of 2 lemons, divided

Juice of 1 lemon

1¼ cups powdered sugar, divided

1½ cups milk

2 eggs

1¼ teaspoons lemon extract

Sliced fresh strawberries (about 2 cups), for garnish

Strawberry Sauce

1 pint fresh strawberries, washed, stemmed, and chopped

⅓ cup sugar

1 teaspoon vanilla

Sweetened Whipped Cream

1 cup heavy whipping cream

⅓ cup powdered sugar

1. Slice the croissants in half lengthwise. Set aside.

2. Combine cream cheese, zest of 1 lemon, strained juice of 1 lemon, and ¾ cup powdered sugar in a medium mixing bowl. Mix with an electric mixer until light and fluffy.

3. Spread lemon cream cheese mixture over the bottoms of croissants and then replace the tops, pressing down to flatten. Cut into halves (or even fourths, if necessary) and arrange the pieces evenly in a 9 x 13-inch pan lightly sprayed with nonstick cooking spray.

4. Whisk together milk, eggs, lemon extract, zest from second lemon, and remaining ½ cup of powdered sugar. Pour evenly over croissants and cover with aluminum foil. Refrigerate 8–10 hours.

5. When ready to bake, preheat oven to 350 degrees F. Bake covered for 30 minutes and then remove foil and bake another 20–30 minutes or until the croissants are golden brown and the liquid is absorbed. Remove from oven and allow to stand 5–10 minutes. Cut into squares and top individual servings with fresh sliced strawberries, Strawberry Sauce, and Sweetened Whipped Cream, if desired.

6. **For the sauce:** Place strawberries and sugar in a large, heavy saucepan. Bring to a simmer over medium heat, stirring frequently. Remove from heat and add vanilla. Crush softened berries with the back of a spoon or a potato masher or, for a smoother sauce, blend using a standard or immersion blender.

7. **For the whipped cream:** Using a hand-held electric mixer, beat cream and sugar on medium-high speed until soft peaks form.

TIP: Extra virgin olive oil can be delicious on salads, but its strong flavor can also overwhelm more delicate flavors such as those we have in this dressing. Light olive oil is a little too mild, so pure olive oil is a good balance between the two—you get the flavor and health benefits of extra virgin olive oil while still being able to taste the other flavors in the dressing.

Balsamic Vinaigrette

Everyone needs a great basic Balsamic Vinaigrette recipe in their collection! This dressing is terrific on a simple salad of baby greens and fresh tomatoes, but it can also be used as a marinade for chicken or beef before grilling.

½ cup pure olive oil (see Tip)

¼ cup balsamic vinegar

2 cloves garlic, minced or pressed

¼ teaspoon black pepper

¼ teaspoon kosher salt

½ teaspoon Creole or mild coarse-grained mustard

½ teaspoon sugar

Combine all ingredients in a jar and shake vigorously until well mixed and then shake well before serving. For a smoother dressing that will not separate, combine all ingredients, except for the oil, in your blender. With the blender running, add the oil in a slow, steady stream.

Strawberry Spinach Salad with Lemon Poppy Seed Vinaigrette

Makes 8–10 side dish servings
or 4 main dish servings

⊕ **Quick and Easy**

ROLLOVER
Red onion

Inexpensive, delicious strawberries are a sure sign that spring is coming! Slice up a handful and toss them in this light, fresh salad. For a cool, quick dinner, add some diced grilled chicken.

1 (10-ounce) bag fresh baby spinach

½–1 small red onion, thinly sliced

1 medium cucumber, seeded and sliced (you can peel it first if you want)

1 pint strawberries, hulled and sliced

1 cup sliced almonds, toasted

½ pound grilled chicken breasts, sliced or diced, optional

For the salad, toss ingredients together and serve immediately. You can also arrange the ingredients on individual plates for serving.

Lemon Poppy Seed Vinaigrette

2–3 large lemons (use as needed to yield ⅓ cup juice and 1 teaspoon zest)

1 teaspoon grated onion

¼ cup rice wine vinegar

¼ cup canola oil

¾ teaspoon kosher salt

¼ teaspoon freshly ground black pepper

¼ cup sugar

2 teaspoons poppy seeds

1 clove garlic, finely pressed

Using a microplane or other fine grater, grate 1 teaspoon lemon zest and 1 teaspoon onion. Place in a small container with a lid. Add remaining ingredients and shake vigorously. If possible, refrigerate at least 1 hour before serving. Shake well before serving.

Mini Tostada Salads

These cute little mini salads make a great appetizer or a fun side dish. They're also perfect finger food for baby or wedding showers.

6–8 small flour tortillas

2 cups shredded romaine lettuce

1 tomato, diced

¼ cup frozen corn, thawed

¼ cup canned black beans, rinsed

2 tablespoons sliced green onions

2 tablespoons chopped cilantro

½ cup shredded or finely diced grilled chicken, optional

Vinaigrette

3 tablespoons white wine vinegar

2 tablespoons canola oil

2 teaspoons honey

⅛ teaspoon kosher salt

2–3 cracks black pepper

½ teaspoon ground cumin

½ teaspoon smoked paprika

½ teaspoon garlic powder

Dash hot sauce

1. Preheat oven to 400 degrees F.

2. Warm tortillas in microwave for 20–30 seconds until soft and pliable. Quickly press each one into the well of a muffin tin or jumbo muffin tin, carefully overlapping the sides if necessary and making the bottom as flat as possible. Bake 10–15 minutes, until golden brown.

3. While tortillas are baking, combine lettuce, tomato, corn, beans, green onions, and cilantro.

4. **For the vinaigrette:** Place all ingredients in a jar with a tight-fitting lid and shake vigorously for 1 minute. Dressing can be prepared up to several days in advance and stored in the refrigerator.

5. When tortillas are done, remove from muffin tin and set on a wire rack to cool. Once cooled completely, toss salad and desired amount of dressing together and fill each tortilla cup.

Author's Note

This unique salad was inspired by my mom, Kathy. The quantities changed, and the ingredients varied depending on what was in the fridge, but the major flavor components stayed the same. She taught me how to adjust recipes depending on what I had on hand. —*Sara*

Kathy's Chicken Salad

Store-bought rotisserie chicken makes this sweet and savory chicken salad even easier! If you've never had mango chutney before, it's like a sweet, tangy, spicy mango jam and can be found with jams and jellies at the grocery store.

2 cups diced cooked chicken

½ cup diced celery

¼ cup sliced green onions

1½ cups shredded or thinly sliced cabbage

⅓ cup dried cranberries

¼ cup chopped fresh cilantro

¼ cup toasted slivered almonds

¼ cup Major Grey's Mango Chutney

¼ cup mayonnaise

½ teaspoon cider vinegar

Kosher salt

Black pepper

Rolls or croissants, optional

Combine chicken, celery, onions, cabbage, cranberries, cilantro, and almonds in a medium-sized bowl. Whisk together the chutney, mayonnaise, and cider vinegar in a small bowl. Add the dressing to the chicken mixture and gently combine. Season with salt and pepper, to taste. For best results, chill at least 30 minutes before serving. If desired, serve on a roll or croissant.

Berry-Kiwi Salad with Mint-Lime Dressing

Serves 6

♥ **Family Favorite**
☺ **Quick and Easy**
🌿 **Vegetarian**

Light, fresh, and easy, this fruit salad comes together in minutes and is an elegant addition to any baby or wedding shower, Mother's Day brunch, or Saturday morning breakfast.

¼ cup freshly squeezed lime juice

2½ tablespoons honey

1 tablespoon finely chopped fresh mint leaves

¾ teaspoon poppy seeds

1 pint strawberries, hulled and sliced

1 cup blackberries

1 cup blueberries

1 cup kiwi, cut into ¼-inch pieces (see Tutorial on kiwi, page 122)

1. Whisk together lime juice, honey, mint leaves, and poppy seeds in a small bowl. Set aside.

2. Gently toss berries and kiwi together in a medium-sized bowl. Drizzle dressing over the fruit and toss gently to combine. Serve immediately.

Easy Thai Coconut Soup

This recipe is proof that great food doesn't have to be expensive or complicated! Whip this up for a last-minute dinner and make it even easier by using leftover or rotisserie chicken.

Serves 4–6

⊙ **Quick and Easy**

ROLLOVERS
Cilantro
Coconut milk
Ginger
Mushrooms

VARIATIONS: Shrimp may be substituted for chicken. Leftover white rice may be substituted for the ramen noodles. For a spicy soup, add a couple of dashes of Sriracha or a pinch of red pepper flakes.

1 teaspoon olive oil

1½ tablespoons minced jalapeño pepper

1½ tablespoons freshly minced ginger, or 1½ teaspoons ground dried ginger

2 (14.5-ounce) cans chicken broth

1 (13.5 ounce) can light coconut milk (about 1¾ cups)

½ teaspoon kosher salt

2 packages ramen noodles (do not use seasoning packet)

¾ cup sliced mushrooms, optional

1½ tablespoons fresh lime juice

1 cup diced or shredded cooked chicken

2 tablespoons chopped cilantro, plus more for garnish

Sliced green onions and lime wedges, for garnish

1. Heat medium-sized soup pot to medium-high heat on stove top. Add oil, jalapeño, and ginger (if using fresh ginger). Cook 1–2 minutes, stirring frequently, until jalapeño and ginger are softened and fragrant. If using ground ginger, add to softened jalapeño and stir. Add chicken broth, coconut milk, and salt and increase heat to bring mixture to a boil. Reduce to simmer and add noodles. Simmer 3–5 minutes, until noodles are softened. If using mushrooms, add them in the final 2–3 minutes of cooking the noodles.

2. Add chicken and simmer about 30 seconds to heat through. Remove pot from heat and stir in lime juice and cilantro. Ladle into serving bowls and garnish with additional chopped cilantro, green onions, and lime wedges, if desired

Split Pea Soup with Ham

If you're searching for ways to use up the rest of your ham after Easter dinner and a few days of ham sandwiches, this healthy and hearty soup may be exactly what you're looking for. Serve this easy, slow-cooker soup with a loaf of crusty bread. Don't forget to add the malt vinegar—it's just a little bit, but it's what makes this soup extra delicious.

1 pound dried split peas, rinsed and sorted

2 quarts chicken or vegetable broth *or* 8 cups water plus 8 teaspoons chicken or vegetable bouillon or soup base

1 pound bone-in ham or ham steak, diced into small pieces and trimmed of excessive fat

2 medium carrots, peeled and chopped

1 medium onion, chopped

4–5 cloves garlic, minced

1 teaspoon Italian seasoning

½ teaspoon marjoram

½ teaspoon smoked paprika

⅛ teaspoon thyme

1 bay leaf

1 teaspoon malt vinegar

Kosher salt, to taste

Freshly ground black pepper, to taste

Sourdough Garlic-Herb Croutons (page 87), optional

Place all the ingredients, except croutons, in a slow cooker and cook 6–8 hours on low or 4 hours on high. You can also cook it on high until it starts to boil and then turn the setting to low until you're ready to serve the soup. Season with salt and pepper, to taste. Top with croutons, if desired.

Serves 8

 **Slow Cooker**

TIP: Ham ends and pieces can be purchased near the other ham cuts or from the butcher. They're very inexpensive and are perfect for this soup because you're cutting up the ham anyway.

⊙ **Quick and Easy**

ROLLOVERS
Celery
Parsley

Author's Note

My kids are much more inter-
ested in eating veggies if they
help grow them in our garden or
pick them out from the farmers'
market. They are always in-
trigued by the brightly colored
rainbow stems of fresh chard,
which makes it extra fun to eat!
—Sara

Chicken Orzo Soup with Lemon and Chard

The brightness of lemon and chard help welcome in spring in this light, healthy soup.

1 tablespoon olive oil

1 large carrot, peeled and sliced

2 ribs celery, sliced

1 medium onion, diced (about 1½ cups)

3 cloves garlic, pressed or minced

3–4 large chard leaves with stems removed and diced, leaves reserved

1 pound boneless, skinless chicken breasts, rinsed in cool water and diced

1½ teaspoons kosher salt

¼ teaspoon freshly ground black pepper

4 cups chicken broth (32 ounces)

½ cup water

½ teaspoon dried oregano

½ teaspoon dried rosemary

1 bay leaf

½ cup orzo pasta

¼ cup chopped fresh parsley

3 tablespoons fresh lemon juice

1. Heat a large stockpot to medium-high heat. Add oil and turn pan to coat surface. Add carrot, celery, onion, garlic, and chard stems. Sauté until vegetables are tender, about 5–6 minutes.

2. While vegetables are cooking, dry chicken with paper towels and sprinkle with salt and pepper. Add chicken to pan and cook until no pink is visible. Add chicken broth, water, oregano, rosemary, and bay leaf. Bring soup to a boil and then reduce to simmer. Cover pot and cook about 20 minutes, stirring occasionally. Add orzo and cook until tender, about 8 minutes. Chop chard leaves (you should have 3–4 cups) and add to pot. Simmer about 2 minutes or until leaves are wilted. Remove from heat; add parsley and lemon juice and stir to combine. If thinner consistency is desired, add additional chicken broth, to taste.

Creamy Roasted Garlic and Asparagus Soup

This light and creamy soup is a subtle and elegant addition to any springtime meal. It's a great accompaniment to sandwiches and salads, or you could even serve it alongside our Spinach-Artichoke Quiche (page 11).

1 head garlic

2 tablespoons extra virgin olive oil, divided

1¼ teaspoons plus ⅛ teaspoon kosher salt, divided

½ teaspoon black pepper, divided

1 pound asparagus (tough ends removed), chopped into 1-inch pieces

2 tablespoons butter

1 medium onion, chopped (about 1 cup)

2 cups milk

¼ cup flour

3 ounces low-fat cream cheese

4 cups chicken broth

1 cup freshly grated Parmesan cheese

1. Preheat oven to 425 degrees F. Remove outer papery skin from garlic head, leaving cloves intact. Slice off top third of garlic head. Discard or save for another use. Place remaining clove on an 8 x 8-inch piece of foil. Drizzle with 1 tablespoon oil and sprinkle with ⅛ teaspoon each of salt and pepper. Pull edges of foil up around garlic and squeeze together at the top. Place foil bundle directly on oven rack and set timer for 15 minutes.

2. Place asparagus on a foil-lined rimmed baking sheet. Toss with remaining tablespoon oil and sprinkle with ¼ teaspoon salt and ⅛ teaspoon pepper. Spread evenly on baking sheet. After garlic has cooked 15 minutes, use a potholder to pick up the foil bundle and place it (still wrapped) on the baking sheet with asparagus. Place baking sheet in oven and roast the asparagus about 20 minutes, or until asparagus is tender and can be easily pierced with a fork.

3. While asparagus and garlic are roasting, heat butter in a large stockpot over medium heat. Add chopped onion and sauté until tender, about 3–4 minutes. While onion is cooking, combine milk, flour, 1 teaspoon salt, ¼ teaspoon pepper, and cream cheese in a blender and process until smooth; add to pot. Cook on medium heat, stirring continuously, until

slightly thickened, about 2–3 minutes. Add chicken broth. Bring to a boil and then reduce heat and cook over medium heat until slightly thickened, about 3–5 minutes.

4. Remove asparagus and garlic from oven. Carefully squeeze the garlic head with your hand and use a spoon to scoop individual garlic cloves and add them into soup pot. Add roasted asparagus and use an immersion blender to blend until smooth. Alternately, place soup in blender and blend in batches until completely smooth and pale green in color. Add Parmesan cheese to the hot soup and stir until smooth. Serve with sandwiches or a salad.

♥ **Family Favorite**
✳ **Freezer Meal**
☆ **Make Ahead**

ROLLOVERS
Cream cheese
Sour cream

FREEZER INSTRUCTIONS:
Prepare as directed in a freezer-safe pan. Cover well with multiple layers of plastic wrap and then foil. Label the foil with baking instructions. When ready to use, either thaw in refrigerator overnight and bake as directed, or place in oven directly from freezer (remember to remove plastic wrap) and bake, covered, about 1 hour, removing foil for last 10 minutes of baking. Let stand 5–10 minutes before serving.

Cheesy Chicken Enchiladas

This is one of Sara's favorite warm comfort foods for chilly days. She splits the batch and places half in an 8 x 8-inch pan for dinner and puts the other half in a freezer pan for an easy weeknight meal another day.

4 tablespoons butter

5 tablespoons flour

2 (15-ounce) cans chicken broth

1½ teaspoons garlic powder

1 teaspoon onion powder

1½ teaspoons cumin

1 teaspoon coriander

1 tablespoon chili powder

⅛ teaspoon black pepper

⅓ cup sour cream

2–3 shakes Tabasco sauce (or similar hot sauce)

Kosher salt, to taste

4 ounces cream cheese

1 (7-ounce) can diced green chiles

3½ cups (about 14 ounces) cooked, shredded chicken

4 cups shredded Monterey Jack or pepper Jack cheese, divided

8–10 medium flour tortillas

1. Preheat oven to 350 degrees F. Lightly spray a 9 x 13-inch pan with non-stick cooking spray and set aside.

2. Melt butter in a large skillet over medium heat. When butter is melted and bubbly, add flour and stir to combine. Continue cooking, whisking continuously until mixture is light golden brown, about 2–3 minutes. Slowly add chicken broth, whisking until smooth. Whisk in garlic powder, onion powder, cumin, coriander, chili powder, and pepper. Bring sauce to a simmer and stir until thickened, 3–4 minutes. Remove from heat and whisk in sour cream and hot sauce. Add salt to taste and set aside.

3. In a separate mixing bowl, soften cream cheese in microwave until it is easily stirred. Add green chiles and ½ cup of reserved sauce. Stir to combine and add chicken and 2 cups Monterey Jack cheese.

4. To make the tortillas easier to roll, place between damp paper towels and microwave 15–20 seconds. Place about ⅓–½ cup chicken mixture on each tortilla and roll tightly. Pour 1 cup sauce into the bottom of prepared pan and spread evenly. Place tortillas snugly in pan. Pour all remaining sauce on top of the tortillas and top with remaining 2 cups cheese. Bake 30–35 minutes, until hot and bubbly throughout and cheese is melted.

⊕ **Quick and Easy**
🌿 **Vegetarian (see Tip)**

ROLLOVERS
Parmesan cheese
Spinach

TIP: For a vegetarian meal, omit bacon and substitute 2 tablespoons melted butter in place of bacon drippings to make the sauce instead.

Cheesy Tortellini Spinach Bake

Spinach and lemon help this dish feel bright and fresh while the tortellini, bacon, and cheese add richness, making it a perfect dinner for a rainy spring afternoon. Add a tossed green salad and a loaf of warm bread to complete this tasty meal.

1 (12-ounce) container cheese or cheese and spinach tortellini

4 ounces bacon or pancetta (see Tip)

3 cloves garlic, pressed or finely minced

2 tablespoons flour

2 cups milk

¾ teaspoon kosher salt

⅛ teaspoon black pepper

1½ teaspoons dried basil

¼ teaspoon red pepper flakes (or more if you prefer a spicier dish)

1 medium lemon

2 cups roughly chopped, loosely packed fresh spinach

¾ cup grated mozzarella cheese, divided

¾ cup grated Parmesan cheese, divided

1. Preheat oven to 350 degrees F. Fill a large stockpot with water and bring to a boil. Add tortellini and cook according to package directions.

2. Cook bacon or pancetta in a medium-sized skillet on medium-high heat until crisp. Remove from pan and set on paper towels to drain. Reserve 2 tablespoons drippings in pan and discard the rest. Add garlic to pan and cook until fragrant and tender, about 1 minute. Add flour to pan and whisk for about 1 minute. Slowly add milk and continue to whisk until smooth. Add salt, pepper, basil, and red pepper flakes and bring sauce to a simmer.

3. While sauce is heating, use a microplane grater or a fine-holed cheese grater to zest the lemon. After zesting the lemon, cut it in half and juice it. Add 2 teaspoons zest and 1 tablespoon lemon juice to sauce. Continue to stir until thickened, 2–3 minutes. Remove from heat.

4. Drain tortellini and return to stockpot. Reserve 1 tablespoon cooked bacon and add the rest to pasta mixture. Add spinach, ½ cup mozzarella cheese, and ½ cup Parmesan cheese. Add sauce and gently stir to combine. Place pasta mixture in an 8 × 8-inch or a 9 × 9-inch baking dish and top with remaining cheeses and crumbled bacon.

5. Cover pan with foil and bake 20 minutes. Remove foil and bake an additional 5–10 minutes, until cheese on top is melted and pasta is bubbly throughout. Remove from oven and cool 10 minutes before serving.

ROLLOVERS
Cilantro
Ginger
Green onions
Mushrooms

TIP 1: To prepare your own ground chicken, cut boneless, skinless chicken breasts into large chunks and pulse in a food processor until ground to a desired consistency.

TIP 2: Sriracha sauce is found in the Asian foods aisle. It has a bright green lid and a picture of a rooster on the bottle. It's delicious and flavorful, but very spicy. In this recipe, 1 teaspoon of Sriracha is quite spicy, so start out with less (or none) and then add it to taste. You could also substitute a traditional hot sauce, such as Tabasco.

Asian Lettuce Wraps

These lettuce wraps are a delicious dinner or appetizer, especially when you're watching your carbs. Kids and adults alike love wrapping the savory meat and veggie filling in a crisp leaf of lettuce!

2 teaspoons canola oil

4 cloves garlic, minced

1 tablespoon minced fresh ginger

1 pound ground chicken (see Tip 1)

3 ounces mushrooms, finely chopped (about 8 small mushrooms)

½ teaspoon kosher salt

4 cups bagged coleslaw mix or thinly shredded cabbage

1 (8-ounce) can sliced water chestnuts, drained, rinsed, and finely minced

½ cup thinly sliced green onions

¼ cup soy sauce

1 teaspoon sesame oil

1 lemon, zested and juiced (you'll need about 3–4 tablespoons juice)

½–1 teaspoon Sriracha or other Asian hot chili sauce (see Tip 2)

⅓ cup roughly chopped cilantro

1–2 heads iceberg lettuce

1. Heat a very large skillet to medium-high heat on the stove top. When hot, add oil and then garlic and ginger. Sauté about 30 seconds, until fragrant, and then add chicken, mushrooms, and salt. Cook about 5 minutes, stirring often, until chicken is cooked through.

2. Add coleslaw mix or cabbage, water chestnuts, and green onions. Cook about 2 minutes, until cabbage starts to wilt. Add soy sauce, sesame oil, lemon zest, lemon juice, and hot sauce, to taste. Remove from heat and stir in cilantro.

3. To serve, carefully remove individual leaves from the head of lettuce (the closer you get to the center, the easier it becomes). If necessary, use a pair of kitchen shears to trim the rough or wilted edges of the lettuce. Spoon the chicken mixture into the leaves and serve with sauce.

Dipping/Drizzling Sauce

4 tablespoons soy sauce

4 tablespoons rice vinegar

3 tablespoons water

2 teaspoons honey

1–2 teaspoons finely minced fresh ginger

For the dipping sauce, whisk all ingredients until well combined.

Quick and Easy Noodle Stir-Fry

⊙ **Quick and Easy**

🌿 **Vegetarian**

ROLLOVERS
Cilantro
Ginger

This recipe is as fast and delicious as take-out! Black sesame seeds aren't necessary, but they're a pretty way to dress this dish up and make it feel as though you were eating from a restaurant. You can customize this dish to your tastes and with what is easily available (or in your freezer).

1 (12-ounce) package linguine noodles (whole wheat or regular)

2–3 teaspoons olive oil

¼ cup soy sauce

2½ tablespoons brown sugar

2½ tablespoons rice wine vinegar

2 tablespoons Asian sweet red chili sauce (we use Thai Kitchen, available with the Asian foods at major grocery stores)

1 tablespoon dark sesame oil

1–2 tablespoons canola or peanut oil, divided

1 small red onion, sliced

4 cloves garlic, minced or pressed

2 tablespoons fresh ginger, minced or pressed

1 cup fresh or frozen green sugar snap peas, snow peas, edamame, or green beans

1 medium zucchini, julienned or chopped

1 large or 2 small orange, red, and/or yellow bell peppers, seeded and sliced

Grilled chicken, shrimp, or steak, optional

Black sesame seeds, chopped cilantro, or lime wedges, optional

1. Bring a large pot of salted water to a boil. Add noodles and cook al dente. When noodles are cooked, drain them and toss in olive oil.

2. Whisk together soy sauce, brown sugar, vinegar, chili sauce, and sesame oil. Set aside.

3. While noodles are cooking, heat canola or peanut oil in a large skillet over high heat. When the oil is hot, add sliced onion, garlic, and ginger. Stir-fry 1–2 minutes or until fragrant, but garlic isn't burning. Add peas (or edamame or beans) and stir-fry about 30 seconds. Add zucchini and peppers and stir-fry another 30 seconds or until veggies are crisp-tender. Add noodles and stir-fry until they are well combined with the vegetables. Give sauce a quick whisk and then drizzle it evenly over noodles and stir-fry entire mixture about 30–60 seconds or until everything is well coated in the sauce. Serve immediately.

4. If desired, add grilled meat to this dish, or garnish individual servings with black sesame seeds, chopped cilantro, and lime wedges.

Serves 4–6

ROLLOVERS
Bell pepper
Cilantro
Ginger

Sweet and Sour Chicken Stir-Fry

This is a perfect dinner that will make your whole family happy on a busy weeknight!

1 tablespoon cornstarch

¼ cup cold water

1 (8-ounce) can pineapple chunks, drained and juice reserved

3 tablespoons ketchup

1 tablespoon soy sauce

2 tablespoons brown sugar

1 teaspoon rice vinegar

3–5 teaspoons vegetable oil, divided

1 pound boneless, skinless chicken breasts or thighs, diced into 1-inch pieces (or pork tenderloin, or sliced boneless pork chops)

½ teaspoon kosher salt

¼ teaspoon black pepper

2 garlic cloves, minced

1 tablespoon minced fresh ginger

3 cups broccoli florets

½ medium bell pepper, cut into ½-inch chunks

½ medium onion, diced

Cooked white or brown rice, for serving

Sesame seeds or chopped fresh cilantro or parsley, for optional garnish

1. Combine cornstarch and water in a medium-sized bowl and stir to dissolve. Add reserved pineapple juice, ketchup, soy sauce, brown sugar, and vinegar to the bowl and stir to combine.

2. Heat 2–3 teaspoons oil in a wok or large, nonstick skillet over medium-high heat. Add chicken, salt, pepper, garlic, and ginger. Stir-fry until chicken is cooked and no longer pink, 3–4 minutes. Remove chicken from pan and cover to keep warm.

3. Add remaining 1–2 teaspoons oil to the pan and add broccoli, bell pepper, and onion. Stir-fry over medium-high heat until vegetables are crisp-tender and broccoli is bright green, about 3–5 minutes.

4. Return chicken to the pan and add pineapple chunks and sauce mixture. Bring to a simmer and cook until everything is heated through and the sauce has thickened, about 1–2 minutes. Season with additional salt and pepper, to taste. Serve over hot cooked rice. If desired, garnish with sesame seeds and chopped fresh cilantro or parsley.

♥ **Family Favorite**
☆ **Make Ahead**

ROLLOVER
Sour cream

TIP: Use a pair of clean kitchen shears to snip the chives.

MAKE-AHEAD INSTRUCTIONS: You can prepare this dish 1–2 days ahead of time and refrigerate it until it's ready to bake. If making baked potatoes earlier in the week, bake up some extras and then use them in this recipe.

Cheesy Garlic and Chive Potatoes

These creamy potatoes are loaded with the fresh spring flavors of garlic and chives. Chives are an easy herb to grow in your garden, and they will produce all summer long. These potatoes are also delicious on any holiday table and are a great addition to a potluck. Serve alongside your favorite steak (page 102) or with burgers.

2 pounds baking potatoes or leftover baked potatoes

1½ cups sour cream

¼ cup freshly chopped chives (or 2 tablespoons dried chives)

3 cloves garlic, pressed

2 tablespoons grated onion

1½ teaspoons kosher salt

¼ teaspoon freshly cracked black pepper

1¼ cups grated sharp cheddar cheese, divided

1¼ cups grated Swiss or Gruyère cheese, divided

1. Cook potatoes a day ahead. Preheat oven to 425 degrees F. Wash potatoes, with skins on, under cold water. Pat dry. Pierce each potato a few times with a knife and then place directly on the oven rack. Bake about 1 hour or until you can easily pierce the potatoes with a knife all the way through. Remove from oven and cool completely. Cover potatoes with plastic wrap and refrigerate until ready to use.

2. When preparing the potatoes the next day, preheat oven to 350 degrees F. Using a large-hole box grater, grate potatoes with skins on. Some of the skin will naturally peel off and you can discard it. Combine sour cream, chives, garlic, onion, salt, and pepper in a large mixing bowl. Add potatoes and gently toss to combine. Add 1 cup cheddar cheese and 1 cup Swiss or Gruyère cheese and fold in to combine. Place mixture in a 1½-quart baking dish, or an 8 x 8-inch baking dish. Sprinkle remaining ½ cup cheddar and Swiss or Gruyère cheeses on top. Sprinkle a few extra chives on top, if desired. Bake 30–40 minutes until hot and bubbly and lightly browned around the edges. Cool 10 minutes before serving.

Lemon-Butter Glazed Carrots

These glazed carrots aren't overly sweet—just a touch of honey combines with butter, fresh lemon, and herbs to make these easy carrots a fresh and beautiful side dish for Easter dinner.

Serves 6–8

☉ **Quick and Easy**

🌿 **Vegetarian**

ROLLOVER
Parsley

1 pound sweet baby carrots

1½ cups water

2 tablespoons butter

2 tablespoons strained fresh lemon juice

1½ teaspoons honey

1 tablespoon minced parsley

Kosher salt, to taste

1. Place carrots and water in a medium-sized pot and heat until water comes to a boil. Reduce heat to a low simmer, cover pot, and cook until carrots are crisp-tender, about 5–8 minutes. While the carrots are cooking, combine the butter, lemon juice, and honey in a small bowl and microwave until the butter is melted and the mixture is smooth.

2. Using a slotted spoon, remove carrots from pot and into a serving bowl. Drizzle the butter mixture over the carrots and toss with the parsley. Season with salt, to taste.

Cinnamon Crème Anglaise

1¾ cups milk

⅓ cup sugar

4 large egg yolks

1 teaspoon pure vanilla

¼ teaspoon ground cinnamon

1. In a small saucepan, heat milk until it nearly boils and then remove from heat and set aside.

2. Whisk sugar and egg yolks together in a medium-sized bowl. Very slowly, add hot milk mixture to the eggs, whisking the entire time. Return the mixture to the pan and cook over medium-low heat until the sauce has thickened and easily coats the back of a spoon. Remove from heat and add vanilla and cinnamon and whisk until distributed.

Bananas Foster Bread Pudding

This bread pudding is a rich, decadent way to use up day-old bread and over-ripe bananas.

4 medium bananas, sliced

2 tablespoons butter, divided

1 cup brown sugar, divided

1 teaspoon cinnamon, divided

1½ cups milk

1½ cups heavy cream

4 eggs

3 egg yolks

1 teaspoon vanilla

¼ teaspoon kosher salt

1½ teaspoons rum flavoring, optional

6 cups day-old bread or croissant cubes

1. Preheat oven to 400 degrees F. Spray a 9 x 13-inch pan with nonstick spray and set aside. Line a rimmed baking sheet with heavy-duty foil. Combine sliced bananas with 1 tablespoon melted butter in a small mixing bowl. Combine ¼ cup brown sugar and ¼ teaspoon cinnamon separately and then add to bananas and butter. Gently toss to combine and spread on the prepared baking sheet. Bake 15 minutes or until bananas are fragrant and tender and the sugar is starting to bubble and caramelize. Remove from oven and reduce heat to 350 degrees F.

2. While bananas are caramelizing, use an electric hand mixer to combine milk, cream, eggs, egg yolks, vanilla, salt, remaining ¾ cup brown sugar, remaining ¾ teaspoon cinnamon, and rum flavoring (if using) in a large mixing bowl. Add bread cubes to the mixture and gently toss to combine. When bananas are done cooking, fold them into the mixture along with any brown sugar and butter left in the pan.

3. Allow to stand 10–15 minutes (longer if possible), folding occasionally so the bread soaks up the egg mixture.

4. Pour mixture into prepared 9 x 13-inch pan and spread evenly. Bake 40–50 minutes or until puffed and golden (but not brown) and a knife inserted into the center comes out clean.

5. Serve with vanilla ice cream, your favorite caramel sauce, or with Cinnamon Crème Anglaise sauce (at left).

Creamy Fruit Mousse

Making and eating this creamy fruit mousse is one of Sara's favorite childhood memories. Use any flavor of gelatin or layer different flavors in one glass.

1 (3-ounce) box fruit-flavored gelatin, regular or sugar free

1 cup boiling water

1 (8-ounce) package cream cheese, divided

½ cup cold water

1 (8-ounce) container whipped topping, divided

½ cup powdered sugar

¼ teaspoon vanilla extract

Zest and juice of 1 small orange

1. Dissolve gelatin in boiling water. Place in blender and add 4 ounces cream cheese. Process until smooth. Add cold water and pulse blender to stir. Add 4 ounces whipped topping (about a heaping cup) to the blender and process until just combined and mixture is free of lumps.

2. Transfer mixture into one serving bowl, or several individual-sized dishes. Refrigerate until firm, about 3–4 hours.

3. Combine remaining 4 ounces cream cheese with powdered sugar, vanilla, 1 teaspoon orange zest (more if desired), and 1 teaspoon fresh orange juice. Beat together until creamy and smooth, and fold in remaining 4 ounces whipped topping. Add more orange juice if needed for consistency.

4. Dollop, pipe, or spread topping over chilled mousse just before serving. Do not refrigerate mousse with the topping on, as it will harden, so it's best to whip it up just before serving.

TIP: Peanut oil is great for frying because it's nearly flavorless and has a high smoke point, but a good alternative is canola oil. When using canola oil, be sure to use fresh oil because food fried in previously used canola oil can take on a fishy taste when it's cooked at high temperatures.

Beignets

Serve these easy and addictive powdered-sugar-dusted pastries alongside a steaming mug of hot chocolate (page 202) and you can almost hear the brass band coming down Decatur Street in New Orleans.

1 cup whole milk	½ cup warm (about 105 degrees F.) water
¼ cup plus 1 tablespoon sugar, divided	3½–4 cups all-purpose flour, divided
¼ cup vegetable oil	1 egg
1 teaspoon salt	Peanut oil for frying
1 scant tablespoon active dry yeast	Powdered sugar

1. Combine milk, ¼ cup sugar, vegetable oil, and salt in a small saucepan. Heat over medium heat until small bubbles form around the edges of the pan. Remove from heat.

2. While the milk mixture is heating, combine yeast and 1 tablespoon sugar with warm water. Allow to stand 10 minutes or until it's very bubbly.

3. Combine heated milk and 2 cups flour in the bowl of a stand mixer. Mix, scraping the bowl occasionally, until smooth (about 2–3 minutes). Add the egg and mix until well combined. Add yeast mixture. Add enough flour to make a soft dough that sticks slightly to your finger.

4. At this point, you can either place the dough in a bowl sprayed with nonstick cooking spray and cover with a piece of sprayed plastic wrap and refrigerate the dough up to 1 day or you can roll the dough out on a lightly floured surface. When ready to use, roll it into a large rectangle about ¼-inch thick. Using a pizza wheel, cut the dough into about 3 x 4-inch rectangles. Slightly separate the dough pieces and cover with a clean cloth. Allow to rise 30 minutes.

5. When the dough has about 15 minutes left to go, heat 2–3 inches peanut oil in a large skillet or saucepan to 325 degrees F. (use a candy thermometer). When oil is heated, fry dough pieces for about 1½ to 2 minutes per side or until they are golden. Carefully remove beignets from oil and allow to drain on a paper-towel-lined baking sheet.

6. Place some powdered sugar in a fine-mesh strainer and sprinkle powdered sugar generously over the beignets. Serve immediately.

Lime-Coconut White Chip Macadamia Nut Cookies

If you're a fan of white chocolate macadamia nut cookies, this tropical version will take you somewhere extra special. A hint of bright citrus and chewy, crunchy coconut will have you on an imaginary tropical island in no time.

2 cups flour, spooned lightly into measuring cups and leveled with knife

½ teaspoon baking soda

½ teaspoon salt

12 tablespoons unsalted butter, melted and cooled until lukewarm

1 cup packed brown sugar

½ cup sugar

1 large egg plus 1 egg yolk

2 teaspoons vanilla extract

1 cup chopped white chocolate or white chocolate chips

1 cup coconut (toasted or untoasted)

1 cup roughly chopped, toasted macadamia nuts

1½–2 tablespoons grated lime zest (1–2 limes)

Makes 2–3 dozen cookies

Author's Note

Our family has a special love for the Hawaiian Islands, and every time we go there we come home with macadamia nuts! I created this cookie so I could have a little taste of the tropics, even on a cold and rainy day in Idaho.
—Sara

1. Heat oven to 325 degrees F. Mix flour, baking soda, and salt together in a medium-sized bowl; set aside.

2. Combine butter and sugars with electric mixer until thoroughly blended. Mix in egg, egg yolk, and vanilla. Add dry ingredients and mix until combined. Add white chocolate chips, coconut, macadamia nuts, and lime zest and stir to distribute.

3. Scoop cookie dough into balls and place 2 inches apart on parchment-lined baking sheets. Bake until cookies are set around outer edges, yet centers are still soft and puffy and appear slightly underbaked, about 9–10 minutes. (All ovens are different, so keep an eye on them!) Cool cookies on cookie sheets for a few minutes and then transfer to a cooling rack. Store in an airtight container up to 2 days.

TIP: A baby spoon works great for filling the cookies with jam. You can also use a zip-top bag with the corner cut off. If using chunky jam, you'll want to puree it first.

Strawberry-Lemon Butter Cookies

This recipe makes a lot of cookies, making it perfect for wedding and baby showers, potlucks, and holiday gift plates.

1 cup real butter, room temperature

⅔ cup sugar

1 lemon, zested and juiced

2 cups all-purpose flour, spooned lightly into measuring cups and leveled with a knife

½ cup strawberry jam

Glaze

1⅓ cups powdered sugar

5–6 teaspoons fresh lemon juice

1–2 drops liquid yellow food coloring, optional

1. Preheat oven to 350 degrees F.

2. Place a cooling rack over a piece of foil or waxed paper and set aside. Using an electric hand mixer or stand mixer, cream butter and sugar for about 1 minute. Add lemon zest (you should have about 1 tablespoon) and mix to combine. Slowly add flour and mix to combine, scraping sides of bowl occasionally.

3. Roll dough into 1-inch balls, which is about ½ tablespoon of dough. Place about 2 inches apart on an ungreased baking sheet. Use your pinkie finger to make an indentation in the center of each cookie and fill with about ¼ teaspoon jam. Bake 9–11 minutes or until just set.

4. Cool 3–4 minutes on pan and then transfer to cooling rack.

5. **For the glaze:** When cookies are completely cool, whisk glaze ingredients together and place in a small zip-top bag. Snip off a very small corner of the bag and drizzle glaze over cookies.

TIP 1: This dessert can be made up to 2 days ahead of time. If making ahead, store in the refrigerator and do not remove from the ramekins until ready to serve.

The longer these finished flans sit, the more the caramel dissolves, forming the sauce. While they can be eaten as soon as they are chilled, for best results, make them at least one day ahead of time.

TIP 2: Some caramel will likely be stuck to your ramekins and also to the pan and spoon you use to prepare it. For easy cleaning, fill pan with hot water immediately after pouring caramel into ramekins and bring it to a simmer on the stove top for a few minutes. Turn off heat and let pan and spoon sit while sugar dissolves and can easily rinse off. Likewise, fill empty ramekins with boiling water and let sit until water cools. Rinse and wash as usual.

Brazilian Caramel Flan

This smooth, creamy Brazilian dessert tastes like crème brûlée, minus the torch. Serve it cold with sweetened whipped cream and toasted coconut. If you're not a fan of coconut, leave it out and increase the vanilla to 1 teaspoon.

¾ cup sugar

1½ tablespoons water

1 teaspoon fresh lemon juice

6 tablespoons shredded coconut, plus additional, if desired, for garnish

1 (14-ounce) can sweetened condensed milk

¾ cup plus 2 tablespoons whole milk (or just use the sweetened condensed milk can to measure)

3 eggs

½ teaspoon pure vanilla extract

1 teaspoon coconut extract

Sweetened whipped cream and toasted coconut for garnish, optional

1. Preheat oven to 325 degrees F.

2. Place a folded dish towel or several folded paper towels in the bottom of a 9 x 13-inch pan. Place 6 (6–8-ounce) ramekins on the towels.

3. Place sugar, water, and lemon juice in a medium-sized pan with at least 3-inch-tall sides. Stir to combine (mixture will be thick). Place pan over medium heat and do not stir again. As mixture melts and comes to a simmer, use a wet pastry brush to wet down the sugar on sides of pan. Do not stir, but occasionally tilt pan to swirl mixture. Simmer sugar until a light amber color is reached, similar to the color of honey—generally 4–6 minutes but sometimes up to 10. Cooking times vary, so watch mixture carefully to avoid scorching. For best results, use a light-colored pan, such as stainless steel, so you can accurately distinguish color. Immediately pour or ladle sugar mixture into each of the ramekins, dividing evenly, and tilt each ramekin to let caramel coat entire surface of bottom of dish. Since caramel hardens quickly, for best results, pour into one or two ramekins at a time and then tilt to coat. If caramel hardens too quickly before tilting ramekin, heat for a few seconds in the microwave to soften. Because caramelized sugar is extremely hot, work carefully.

4. When all the caramel has been poured, sprinkle 1 tablespoon shredded coconut on top of caramel layer in each ramekin.

5. Place sweetened condensed milk, whole milk, eggs, vanilla, and coconut extract in a blender and process until smooth. Pour mixture into ramekins, dividing mixture evenly and filling close to the top.

6. Place the 9 x 13-inch pan on oven rack and then add hot water to it, being careful not to spill any inside the ramekins. Fill so water reaches halfway to three-fourths up the sides of the ramekins. Bake 50–60 minutes, or until toothpick inserted an inch from the edge comes out clean. The middles should be slightly jiggly. Remove pan from oven and let sit 10–15 minutes.

7. Carefully remove ramekins and let cool on a rack until they reach room temperature. Cover each one with plastic wrap and refrigerate a minimum of 8 hours, but preferably overnight. To serve, run a sharp knife between edge of ramekin and flan and then invert onto a small plate, shaking lightly if needed. Spoon as much caramel as possible onto the top. If desired, top with a little sweetened whipped cream and a garnish of toasted coconut.

Author's Note

While living in Brazil, I absolutely fell in love with Brazilian-style caramel flan. I learned from the locals how to make the traditional dish, known as *pudim de leite*, generally cooked in a tube pan and sliced. My version adds another classic Brazilian flavor, coconut, and is made in individual-sized ramekins. It's the perfect ending for any Latin-inspired meal, and a bonus is that it can be made a day ahead of time. —*Sara*

♥ Family Favorite

Author's Note

This cake is a family favorite from my childhood. My grown brother still requests it every year for his birthday! It's so easy to prepare, yet tastes incredibly decadent. You can also replace the pudding and milk with a small (3-ounce) box of lemon gelatin and water. —Sara

Glazed Lemon Cake

A bright and sunny cake topped with a sweet lemony glaze, this cake is incredibly easy and sure to become a family favorite!

1 (18.25-ounce) box yellow cake mix

1 (3.4-ounce) box lemon instant pudding

¾ cup milk

¾ cup vegetable oil

4 eggs

6 tablespoons real butter, melted

6 tablespoons fresh lemon juice

3 cups powdered sugar

Prepared whipped topping or sweetened whipped cream for serving

1. Preheat oven to 350 degrees F. Spray a 9 x 13-inch pan with nonstick cooking spray and set aside.

2. Ignore ingredients on cake mix and pudding boxes. Combine dry cake mix, dry pudding mix, milk, oil, and eggs. Beat 30 seconds on low speed, scrape edges of bowl, and beat 2 minutes on medium-high speed. Pour into a 9 x 13-inch baking pan and bake according to cake mix box instructions, increasing time if necessary, until a skewer inserted into cake comes out clean.

3. When cake is almost finished baking, combine melted butter, lemon juice, and powdered sugar and whisk until smooth. When cake is baked, use a skewer or large fork to poke holes all over hot cake. Pour glaze over cake and let soak into holes. If desired, reserve a small amount of glaze to drizzle over finished pieces of cake. Let cake cool to room temperature, or chill, if desired. Cut into squares and serve with whipped cream.

Makes 8 cups

♥ **Family Favorite**

TIP: This treat can be made with any flavor gelatin to fit any holiday. Experiment with different flavors to find your favorite. (We love strawberry and lime!) Be aware, however, that some colors, such as blue, might change color during the baking process.

St. Patrick's Day Popcorn

If you think gelatin is just for old-school church dinners, you have to try it as a "candy" coating for your popcorn! This salty, fruity treat will be a hit with big and little kids alike. We love green for St. Patrick's Day, but try it with red gelatin for Christmas, or shades of pink for Valentine's Day!

8 cups popped popcorn

¼ cup butter

3 tablespoons light corn syrup (honey is a good substitute)

½ cup sugar

1 (3-ounce) box lime gelatin, such as Jell-O, or any other flavor (*not* sugar-free)

1. Preheat oven to 300 degrees F. Line a jelly roll pan with foil or parchment. If using foil, spray lightly with nonstick cooking spray and set aside. Place popcorn in an extra-large mixing bowl.

2. Combine butter and syrup in a saucepan over medium heat. Stir until butter is melted. Add sugar and gelatin and stir to combine.

3. Increase heat and bring to a boil. Reduce heat and simmer 5 minutes.

4. After the sugar mixture has simmered, immediately (and carefully) pour over the popcorn in the bowl. Mix immediately and continue stirring until the popcorn is well coated. Spread the mixture evenly onto the prepared pan.

5. Place the pan in the oven and bake for about 10 minutes.

6. Remove the pan from the oven and allow it to cool to room temperature.

7. Break the popcorn into pieces and enjoy!

Chocolate Cupcakes

These super-quick, one-bowl cupcakes are light, fudgy, and the perfect choco-
late base for your favorite cupcake decorations. Use them in our Peppermint
Fudge Cupcake Jars (page 240) or our S'mores Cupcakes (page 131).

½ cup sugar

½ cup packed brown sugar

¼ cup plus 2 tablespoons unsweetened
    cocoa powder

¾ cup all-purpose flour, lightly spooned
    into measuring cups and leveled

1 teaspoon baking soda

½ teaspoon baking powder

½ teaspoon salt

1 egg

½ cup buttermilk

½ cup canola oil

½ teaspoon vanilla

½ cup boiling water

1. Heat oven to 350 degrees F. Line muffin tin with baking cups.

2. Combine sugars, cocoa, flour, baking soda, baking powder, and salt in a
   large bowl. Add egg, buttermilk, oil, and vanilla and combine. Add water
   and beat on medium speed for 2 minutes. The batter will be thin. Fill
   cups three-fourths full with batter.

3. Bake 15–20 minutes or until a toothpick inserted into the center comes
   out clean. Cool completely and decorate as desired.

**Makes 12 jumbo cupcakes
or 14–16 standard-sized
cupcakes**

☆ **Make Ahead**

ROLLOVER
Buttermilk

TIP: These cupcakes are super moist,
so they won't dry out if you need to
make them a day ahead of time.

VARIATION: To make the Cherry
Chocolate Cupcakes (shown below), dip
the tops of baked and cooled cupcakes
in ganache (use the ganache recipe
on page 240 minus the peppermint
extract), and frost with our Simple
Buttercream Frosting (page 58) mixed
with 1 cup pitted diced fresh cherries
and one teaspoon almond extract. Top
with a fresh cherry if desired.

ROLLOVER
Cream

Tres Leches Cupcakes

Cupcakes are a fun twist on this traditional Mexican recipe, and they are perfect for Cinco de Mayo. Be sure to bake these in foil liners so the sweet milk drizzled over the cupcakes doesn't ruin your fiesta!

1 recipe Easy Vanilla Cupcakes using a white cake mix (page 56)

1 cup evaporated milk

1 (14-ounce) can sweetened condensed milk

2 cups heavy cream, divided

3–4 tablespoons caramel syrup

Sliced fresh fruit, such as strawberries, mangoes, and kiwis, optional

Juice of 1 lime, optional

1. Bake cupcakes in foil liners according to recipe directions. Foil liners are extremely important because they help contain the milk mixture.

2. After cupcakes have cooled, use a bamboo skewer to poke several holes in each cupcake. Set aside.

3. Whisk together evaporated milk, sweetened condensed milk, and ¾ cup cream in a medium-sized bowl. Hold a cupcake over the milk mixture and, using a ladle, pour the mixture over the cupcake, letting excess run back into the bowl. Use several spoonfuls on each cupcake and continue until all cupcakes are moistened. Repeat until entire milk mixture is used up. Refrigerate cupcakes until ready to serve.

4. When ready to serve, beat remaining 1¼ cups cream until medium peaks form. Gently fold in caramel syrup and pipe or dollop whipped cream on each of the cupcakes. If desired, toss sliced fruit with lime juice and top cupcakes with sliced fruit. Serve on a small plate with a dessert spoon.

♥ **Family Favorite**

☺ **Quick and Easy**

ROLLOVERS
Greek yogurt
Sour cream

TIP: The sour cream makes these cupcakes incredible, so don't leave it out. You can use full-fat or light sour cream, but fat-free sour cream has too much water and the cupcakes won't bake properly if you use it. However, you can use fat-free plain Greek yogurt, which is almost identical in flavor and texture to full-fat sour cream.

Easy Vanilla Cupcakes

We often get asked if cupcakes that use a cake mix can really be that delicious and we promise, they can! We start with a high-quality cake mix for these cupcakes because they are consistently fabulous regardless of elevation. Plus, a little sour cream never hurt anybody.

1 (18.25-ounce) white or yellow cake mix (we prefer Duncan Hines)

1 cup sour cream or plain Greek yogurt (see Tip)

3 eggs

½ cup canola oil

1 teaspoon vanilla extract

1 teaspoon almond extract

1. Preheat oven to 350 degrees F. Line two 12-cup muffin tins with cupcake liners and set aside.

2. Combine all ingredients in a large bowl or the bowl of your stand mixer and beat 30 seconds on medium speed or until the mixture is moistened. Increase the speed to high and beat another 3 minutes. Divide the batter evenly among the lined muffin tins.

3. Bake 15–18 minutes or until golden on top and a toothpick inserted into the center of one of the cupcakes comes out clean. Allow to cool completely and then decorate as desired.

Peanut Butter Cup Cupcakes

Made from a doctored-up cake mix, these cupcakes are unbelievably easy and just as delicious. We combine two of our favorite frostings and swirl them together for the ultimate presentation. We guarantee you'll earn super-cool points from the kids in your life for making these.

1 (18.25-ounce) yellow or white cake mix (we prefer Duncan Hines)

1 cup sour cream (full-fat or light, but not fat-free)

3 eggs

¼ cup canola oil

¾ cup creamy peanut butter

1 teaspoon vanilla

24 unwrapped mini Reese's Peanut Butter Cups

½ recipe Chocolate Frosting (page 58)

½ recipe Peanut Butter Frosting (page 59)

Makes 24 cupcakes

♥ Family Favorite

ROLLOVER
Sour cream

TIP: Evaporated milk adds a lot of richness to frostings without additional fat. If you don't have any on hand, regular milk will work, too.

1. Preheat oven to 350 degrees F. Line two 12-cup muffin tins with cupcake liners and set aside.

2. Combine all cupcake ingredients, except the peanut butter cups, in a large bowl. Using an electric mixer on medium-low speed, mix for 30 seconds, scraping the bowl frequently. Turn the speed to high and beat another 3 minutes.

3. Fill each muffin cup halfway with batter. Top with an unwrapped Reese's Peanut Butter Cup and then add remaining batter. Make sure the peanut butter cups are covered and the muffin cups are about three-fourths full. Bake 18–22 minutes or until tops are golden. Remove from oven and allow to cool completely.

4. While the cupcakes are cooling, prepare the frostings. For both frostings, combine all the ingredients for each one and whip until light and fluffy, adding additional milk as needed. To frost the cupcakes, see the tutorial on How to Make Swirled, Multicolored Frosting on page 60.

Frostings

Marshmallow Frosting (pictured at top left)

¾ cup real butter (see Tip 1), room
   temperature

¾ cup powdered sugar

1 teaspoon vanilla extract

1 (7-ounce) container marshmallow
   cream

3–5 tablespoons milk or cream, as needed

Beat butter, powdered sugar, and vanilla extract until creamy and smooth. Use a stand mixer with a paddle attachment if you have one. Add marshmallow cream and blend until incorporated. Scrape sides of bowl and continue beating a full minute at medium-high speed. Add milk, one tablespoon at a time, and beat until combined. When you add milk, frosting may change in appearance and appear clumped and separated. Continue beating on high speed until it comes back together and appears fluffy and smooth. Repeat with tablespoons of milk until desired consistency is reached.

Chocolate Frosting

½ cup melted butter (no substitutions)

¼ cup plus 2 tablespoons unsweetened
   cocoa powder

1 pound powdered sugar

¼ cup plus 2 tablespoons evaporated milk

1 teaspoon vanilla extract

Beat the ingredients together on medium speed until light and fluffy.

Simple Buttercream Frosting

1 cup unsalted butter, at room temperature (no substitutions)

1 pinch salt

3 cups powdered sugar

4–6 tablespoons cream or milk, more or
   less as needed

1½ teaspoons vanilla extract (see Tip 2)

Almond (our favorite), lemon, or peppermint extract, to taste, optional

Beat butter until smooth and creamy, about 1 minute. Use a wire mesh strainer to sift powdered sugar into large mixing bowl. Add butter to powdered sugar. Beat on low speed until combined and then on medium-high speed for a full minute. Add extracts. Reduce speed and add milk, one tablespoon at a time, beating well after each addition, until desired consistency is reached. Beat on medium-high speed until light and fluffy.

For Chocolate Buttercream Frosting (pictured at left), add ⅓–½ cup unsweetened cocoa powder, to taste, and additional cream as needed.

TIP 1: Using salted butter in this recipe results in a noticeably salty flavor, which contrasts well with sweet cupcakes. If you'd rather control the amount of salt yourself, use unsalted butter and add a pinch of salt when you beat it with the powdered sugar.

Cream Cheese Frosting

2 (8-ounce) packages cream cheese (light works fine, although it will yield a slightly softer frosting), at almost room temperature

½ cup salted butter, at almost room temperature

1 teaspoon vanilla or almond extract

2 cups sifted powdered sugar

1. Whip cream cheese, butter, and extract together until light and fluffy.

2. Add in the powdered sugar and whip until smooth and fully incorporated. Refrigerate any leftovers (or anything you've frosted that doesn't get eaten immediately).

Mild Cream Cheese Frosting

1 (8-ounce) package cream cheese

1 cup butter (no substitutions)

3½ cups powdered sugar

½ teaspoon vanilla extract

2–4 tablespoons milk or cream

Beat all ingredients, except milk, together on medium-high speed until light and fluffy. If needed, add milk until desired consistency is reached.

Peanut Butter Frosting

1 cup creamy peanut butter

½ cup butter, softened (no substitutions)

4 cups powdered sugar

2 teaspoons vanilla extract

4–6 tablespoons (or more) of milk

Beat ingredients together on medium-high speed until light and fluffy.

Sweetened Whipped Cream (pictured at right)

1 cup cream or heavy cream

⅓ cup powdered sugar

1 teaspoon vanilla extract, optional

Combine all ingredients in a large bowl. With an electric hand mixer, beat mixture until soft peaks form. Serve immediately.

ROLLOVER
Cream

TIP 2: Using butter and vanilla will create a frosting that is off-white in color. If you'd like a whiter color, use clear vanilla, found in baking supply and craft stores.

How to Make Swirled, Multicolored Frosting

TIP: If you can't find large couplers and tips at a department store, they are easily found at craft stores or online.

Up to 4 colors and/or flavors of frosting

1 frosting bag for each color and/or flavor of frosting, plus 1 to place them all in

1 large frosting bag coupler

1 large frosting tip, such as Wilton 1M or 2D

1. Partially fill each icing bag with a different flavor or color of frosting. If you are using 2 flavors, fill each about one-half full. For 3 flavors, fill the bags about one-third full and for 4 flavors, fill each bag one-fourth of the way full.

2. Place the bags on a flat surface and flatten out the frosting slightly and then stack the frosting bags on top of each other.

3. Fit the remaining bag with the large coupler.

4. Cut about ½ inch off the tips of the stacked bags. Slip the stack of frosting bags into the bag fitted with the large coupler.

5. Holding the outer bag firmly to ensure the frosting stays in the bags, squeeze the bag long enough to make sure all of the colors are coming out of the bag.

6. Using steady pressure and a single motion, frost the cupcakes by placing the tip on the outside edge of the cupcake and circling around, overlapping slightly, until you have reached the center of the cupcake. When you reach the center, release pressure and lift up.

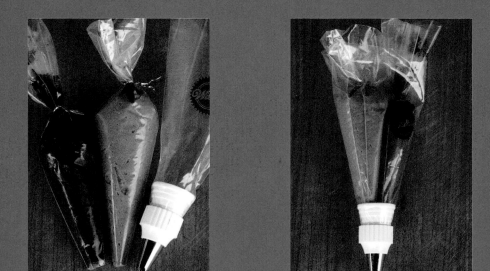

Easy Chick Cupcakes

Makes 24 cupcakes

These cupcakes require little-to-no cake decorating ability, and the ingredients are all inexpensive and easy to find! If you don't like coconut, you can always use yellow sprinkles.

1 recipe Easy Vanilla Cupcakes (page 56)

Frosting of your choice (see page 58 for some of our favorites)

1½ cups shredded coconut or yellow sprinkles, optional

2–3 drops yellow food coloring (for the coconut), optional

Orange Starbursts, Tootsie Rolls, or other soft, moldable candy

Mini M&M's

1. Make cupcake and frosting recipes according to directions.

2. If using coconut, mix the coconut and food coloring and stir with a fork until color is evenly distributed. Set aside.

3. Cut the orange candy into small pieces and mold into beak shapes.

4. Frost the cupcakes (tint frosting yellow, if desired) and cover with coconut. Place 2 M&M's on the cupcakes for the eyes and add a candy beak.

Author's Note

Our favorite thing to do with dinosaur eggs? Have a dinosaur picnic with dinosaur egg salad sandwiches! —Sara

Dinosaur Eggs

If your kids are anything like ours, they love "science experiments." And dinosaurs. These eggs aren't just unbelievably cool, they're also edible, which may be the only way we'll ever get our kids to eat hard-boiled eggs!

Hard-boiled eggs

Liquid food coloring

Small cups or bowls

Water

1. After you've cooked (and cooled) your eggs, gently tap each egg over the countertop or table to create cracks over the entire shell. You can even gently squeeze the egg to create cracks. It's okay if a few pieces come off, but try to keep the shell as intact as possible.

2. Fill individual cups with water if you'd like to color each egg a different color, or use a bowl of water to color several eggs the same color. Add about 6–8 drops food coloring per 1 cup water. You can add less for a lighter color or more for intense color. Refrigerate eggs in the cups or bowls overnight.

3. In the morning, remove the eggs from the water and rinse them well. Gently remove the shells and enjoy your dinosaur eggs!

Easy Bird's Nest Treats

These fun little edible bowls are a great way to showcase egg-shaped Easter candy, such as chocolate eggs or jelly beans.

1 (5-ounce) can crunchy chow mein noodles

1¼ cups white chocolate chips

1 teaspoon vegetable oil

½ cup toffee bits

Chocolate eggs or jelly beans

Makes 18 nests

1. Place chow mein noodles in a medium mixing bowl and set aside.

2. Place white chocolate chips and vegetable oil in a microwave-safe bowl. Heat 30 seconds, stir, and heat in additional 15-second intervals until mixture is melted and smooth. Pour chocolate mixture over chow mein noodles and quickly sprinkle toffee on top. Stir until all chow mein noodles are coated. Drop about 2 tablespoons of mixture into mounds on waxed paper or parchment paper and shape into nests. Add candies to the centers.

Carrot Napkin Bundles

If you're having lots of guests for Easter dinner or brunch, the last thing you want to do (or at least the last thing we want to do) is wash a lot of dishes. Keep things festive by setting the table with these adorably easy packets of knives, forks, and spoons!

Large orange napkins

Green plastic cutlery

Fasteners (ribbon, twine, twist ties, pipe cleaners, etc.)

1. Unfold the napkin as shown at left, with the opening at the top.

2. Take the bottom right-hand corner and fold it to the middle of the napkin.

3. Place cutlery on the opposite side. We put the knife in back and the fork on top of the spoon, partially because the fork sits in the spoon nicely, and partially because we like that the fork looks the most like a carrot top!

4. Start rolling from left-hand side and roll the cutlery right up to the middle.

5. Grab the other side of the triangle and roll it the rest of the way around so you have a nice little carrot-shaped bundle

6. Fasten the bundles with ribbon or twine—green ribbon is a perfect touch!

7. Place a carrot bundle by each plate or lay them together in a basket for a great Easter centerpiece!

Herb-Dyed Easter Eggs

Head out into your backyard to snip herbs, flowers, grasses, and leaves for these beautiful and easy Easter eggs that cost next to nothing! Using liquid food coloring lets you mix, match, and customize the colors exactly the way you want them.

Hard-boiled eggs

Liquid food coloring

White vinegar

Inexpensive nylon stockings

Twist ties

Fresh flat-leafed herbs (such as parsley, cilantro, or tarragon) or other flowers, grasses, or sprigs from the garden

1. For each color of dye, combine 1 cup of water, 1 teaspoon vinegar, and 5–10 drops of liquid food coloring in a small bowl.

2. Cut nylon into squares large enough to cover an egg completely. Keep in mind that the nylons will stretch quite a bit, so make sure the pieces fit tightly against the eggs.

3. Lay a square of nylon on a flat surface and arrange the herbs or leaves on top. Lay an egg down on top of the herbs and carefully wrap the nylon around the entire egg so the herbs stay between the egg and the nylon. Rearrange herbs if necessary and then use a twist tie to tightly secure the nylon. Place the wrapped eggs in prepared dye and let sit until desired color is achieved. Remove and gently blot with a paper towel before removing nylon and herbs. Keep refrigerated until ready to use or display.

Grass-Filled Easter Eggs

Start working on these adorable kid-friendly crafts three weeks before Easter so the grass can grow in completely! These can be used as a fresh, earthy Easter centerpiece.

Sharp knife

Eggs

Potting soil

¼ teaspoon grass seed per egg

Googly eyes, pipe cleanerts, construction paper, and scissors, optional

1. With a small, sharp knife, carefully puncture the top of an egg and gently break off the top one-third of the shell. Pour out egg and reserve for cooking. Carefully wash egg shells and pat dry.

2. Fill shells ¾ full with potting soil and sprinkle in about ¼ teaspoon grass seed. Sprinkle a small amount of soil on top of the seeds and drizzle in a little water.

3. Place eggs in a sunny spot and watch grass sprout and grow! As grass fills in and gets tall, trim with scissors. If desired, decorate faces on eggs and add pipe cleaner feet for little chicks.

TIP: Next time you have a recipe that calls for eggs, carefully open from the top and save the shell for this project. Plastic eggs can be used as well.

Author's Note

Kids are fascinated by the idea of planting something and watching it grow. I love to do large groupings of these eggs in cute containers. If you don't have egg holders, try nestling them in a basket filled with moss or stones. It makes a wonderful living centerpiece! —Sara

67

Fruit Pizza, see page 120

Summer

FATHER'S DAY

Fourth of July

WHAT WE LOVE

- longer days in the sun
- warmer nights under the stars
- crickets chirping
- cicadas buzzing
- bowls of homemade ice cream
- melting Popsicles
- running through the sprinklers
- hot dogs cooked over a campfire
- ice-cold watermelon
- steaks and burgers sizzling on the grill
- parties with friends and family
- being a kid again

IN SEASON

Bell peppers, blackberries, blueberries, cherries, cucumbers, grapes, kiwi, peaches, raspberries, summer squash, sweet corn, tomatillos, tomatoes, watermelon, zucchini

SUMMER

Tropical Smoothie

In Louisiana, where Kate lives, everyone hits a point in the summer when the only things they want to eat are frozen. Pineapple sherbet and cream of coconut give this smoothie an indulgent, tropical feel.

1½ cups orange-mango-peach juice

½ cup cream of coconut

1 cup cubed mangoes or peaches

1 cup raspberries or strawberries

1½ cups (about 3 large scoops) pineapple sherbet

2 cups ice (if using frozen fruit, omit 1 cup ice for each cup frozen fruit)

Add all ingredients to your blender in the order listed and process until smooth. Drink immediately.

Makes 4 small or 2 large smoothies

TIP: Cream of coconut is a thick, sweetened coconut milk available with the cocktail supplies in any grocery store. It is packaged in cans or squeeze bottles; be sure to shake it very well before using. Leftovers can be frozen for future use.

How to Make Fruit Smoothies

Getting the proportions of smoothie ingredients just right can be kind of a challenge, but follow this guide and you can mix and match with any flavors you want! These measurements will make about 3 small smoothies, 2 large smoothies, or 1 very large smoothie.

1. Choose 1 item from Base 1 (juice OR milk; don't combine the two!).
2. Choose 1 item from Base 2.
3. Balance out your fruits. You aren't limited to 2 fruits, but you do need to make sure the flavors balance out; don't use more than ¾ cup total of a strong fruit or 1 cup total of a moderate fruit, but you can mix and match within a category to equal the ¾ cup or 1 cup total.
4. Choose any extra add-ins.

BASE #1

- 1 cup juice
- Apple juice (a good, neutral flavor)
- Cranberry juice (strong and distinct)
- Orange juice (Use a high-quality, not-from-concentrate juice, such as Simply Orange, for really yummy results.)
- Orange-peach-mango juice (great for tropical smoothies or where you want just a hint of citrus)
- Passion fruit juice (If you can find it, it makes great tropical smoothies.)
- Pineapple juice
- Pomegranate juice (strong and distinct)
  Or . . .
  1 cup milk, chocolate milk, soy milk, almond milk, coconut milk, or kefir

BASE #2

- 6–8 ounces yogurt. Vanilla is a great neutral base, but you can use any flavored yogurt as well
- 1 very generous scoop of vanilla or chocolate frozen yogurt or ice cream
- 1 very generous scoop of any flavor of sherbet or sorbet
- 1 cup crushed ice (Buy a bag of pebble ice at restaurants, such as Sonic, that use that kind of ice because it blends to a smooth, fine consistency.)
- 1 cup soft tofu, drained
- 1 cup cream of coconut

EXTRA ADD-INS

- Protein powder
- 1–2 handfuls of baby spinach (Sounds weird, but it's seriously so good and a great way to get your kids to eat leafy greens; you can't even taste it!)
- Sweeteners as needed: honey, sugar, 1–2 packets Splenda, etc., to taste
- Flavorings and spices, such as vanilla, almond, cinnamon, nutmeg, cloves, ginger, etc.
- Peanut butter (1–2 tablespoons)

FRUIT

- 1½ cups mild fruit: peaches, cubed honeydew, or cantaloupe
- 1 cup moderate-flavored fruit: strawberries, cubed mangoes, frozen pineapple chunks, or blackberries
- ¾ cup strong-flavored fruit: 1 small frozen banana, raspberries, or blueberries

POSSIBLE FLAVOR COMBINATIONS

1 cup orange-peach-mango or passion fruit juice
1 very generous scoop pineapple sherbet
1½ cups peaches
1 cup mango

• • •

1 cup orange juice
1 very generous scoop pineapple sherbet
¾ cup blueberries
1 cup strawberries

• • •

2 cups orange juice
1 cup strawberries
1 small banana (Add 1 cup ice if using a fresh, nonfrozen banana or if omitting the banana.)
Spinach

• • •

1 cup apple juice
1 cup vanilla yogurt
1 cup strawberries
1 small banana (or another cup of strawberries)

• • •

½ cup milk
½ cup ice
1 generous scoop vanilla frozen yogurt or vanilla ice cream
2 cups blackberries or raspberries

⊙ **Quick and Easy**
🌱 **Vegetarian**

ROLLOVERS
Cilantro
Red onion

Peach-Watermelon Salsa

Try serving this sweet, spicy salsa with tortilla chips or fire up the grill and serve it on top of your favorite grilled steak or chicken.

4 peaches, peeled and diced

1 cup diced watermelon

1 small jalapeño pepper, seeded and minced (about 1 tablespoon minced)

4 Roma tomatoes, seeded and diced

1 orange bell pepper, seeded and diced

½ cup diced red onion

½ cup chopped fresh cilantro

½ teaspoon sugar

½ teaspoon kosher salt

⅛ teaspoon black pepper

1 medium lime, zested and juiced

Combine peaches, watermelon, jalapeño, tomatoes, bell pepper, red onion, and cilantro. Add sugar, salt, pepper, and the zest and juice of the lime. Toss to combine and chill a minimum of 1 hour. Toss again before serving.

Roasted Tomatillo Salsa

This tangy salsa gets all its zing from the tomatillos, which taste surprisingly like limes. Roasting the tomatillos helps bring out some of their natural sweetness. Serve this salsa with tortilla chips or with your favorite Mexican food.

1 pound tomatillos, husks removed

3–4 cloves garlic, unpeeled

1 small yellow or white onion, peeled and quartered

1 jalapeño pepper (membranes and seeds removed), cut in half lengthwise

1 tablespoon olive oil

¾ teaspoon kosher salt

½ teaspoon freshly ground black pepper

Juice of 1 lime

½ cup chopped cilantro

¼–⅓ cup chopped green onions

ROLLOVERS
Cilantro
Green onions

TIP: Tomatillos look like small, bright green tomatoes inside a papery husk. You'll generally find them either near the tomatoes or the jalapeños and other Mexican peppers. Use tomatillos that feel firm and unshriveled and aren't overly sticky. Also, buy more than you think you'll need to account for the weight of the husks and in case you run into some bad tomatillos.

1. Preheat oven to 500 degrees F. Line a baking sheet with aluminum foil and set aside.

2. After husking the tomatillos, rinse them well in cool water (they may be sticky). Cut the stems and hard portions (if any) off the tomatillos and cut any large ones in half.

3. Place tomatillos, unpeeled garlic, onion, and jalapeño on the lined baking sheet. Drizzle with oil and toss the ingredients with your hands to make sure they are all well coated.

4. Bake vegetables 15 minutes. If they have not charred, turn the broiler on to high and cook 3–5 more minutes or until the skins of the peppers and tomatillos begin to turn black. Remove from oven and allow to cool.

5. When vegetables have cooled, carefully squeeze the skin of the roasted garlic, releasing the soft, roasted garlic clove into a blender or food processor. Add remaining roasted vegetables and then add salt, pepper, and lime juice. Process until the desired consistency is reached and then transfer to a serving dish. Stir in chopped cilantro and green onions and serve.

☺ **Quick and Easy**
🌿 **Vegetarian**

ROLLOVERS
Basil
Red onion

TIP: If preparing ahead of time, wait to add basil until just before serving.

Bruschetta

This fresh and easy Italian appetizer can double as a light meal on hot summer nights, especially if you add a slice of fresh mozzarella.

2 cups diced Roma or fresh garden tomatoes, seeded

⅓ cup diced red onion

1½ teaspoons balsamic vinegar

¼ teaspoon kosher salt

2–3 cracks black pepper

1 teaspoon extra virgin olive oil, plus more for brushing on the bread

¼ cup chopped fresh basil leaves

1 French baguette or crusty bread of your choice

1–2 large garlic cloves

Fresh mozzarella cheese, optional

1. Preheat oven to 400 degrees F.

2. Combine tomatoes, onion, vinegar, salt, pepper, and 1 teaspoon olive oil in a bowl and mix to combine. Add basil and gently toss until combined. Taste and add more salt and pepper, if necessary. Cover and chill.

3. Slice baguette into ½-inch slices and place on a baking sheet. Lightly brush a little oil on the bread slices. Place in oven for 8–10 minutes until just lightly toasted. Remove pan from oven. Slice garlic clove(s) in half and rub the cut side of garlic on the top of each piece of bread. Top with about 1 tablespoon of the tomato mixture.

4. If desired, place one slice of mozzarella cheese on bread before topping with tomato mixture. The cheese is delicious cold, or you can also place the pan back into the oven under the broiler and allow the cheese to melt and become bubbly before adding the tomato mixture on top.

One-Bowl Zucchini Banana Muffins

These muffins are packed with zucchini and dotted with spice. The addition of a banana makes them velvety soft and adds a perfect hint of sweetness. Whisking the dry ingredients right in the mixing bowl minimizes dirty dishes, leaving you with more time for the important things in life, like eating more muffins.

Makes 12 muffins

♥ **Family Favorite**
☻ **Quick and Easy**

½ cup butter, melted

½ cup packed brown sugar

¼ cup sugar

1 large egg

2 teaspoons vanilla

1½ cups all-purpose flour

1 teaspoon baking soda

1 teaspoon ground cinnamon

⅛ teaspoon ground nutmeg

1 medium banana, mashed (about ⅓ cup)

1½ cups grated zucchini

1. Preheat oven to 350 degrees F. Line 12 muffin cups with paper liners and set aside.

2. Melt butter in a microwave-safe mixing bowl. Add sugars, egg, and vanilla, and stir to combine.

3. Lightly spoon flour into measuring cup and level with a knife. Add to mixing bowl, but do not stir. Sprinkle baking soda, cinnamon, and nutmeg over flour. Using a whisk, lightly stir dry ingredients together and then use a rubber spatula to stir just until flour mixture is incorporated into batter. Add mashed banana and zucchini and stir until combined.

4. Divide batter evenly into muffin cups, filling about three-fourths full or a little fuller. Bake 15–20 minutes or until a toothpick comes out with only small crumbs attached.

Naan (Indian-Style Flatbread)

This individually sized flatbread is great for serving with Indian food. It can be cooked over direct heat, on the grill, on a grill pan, or even in a panini press.

1 cup warm water (105–110 degrees F.)

¼ cup sugar

1 package rapid-rise yeast (2¼ teaspoons)

3½–4 cups all-purpose flour, divided

2 teaspoons salt

1 egg, room temperature, lightly beaten

¼ cup plain yogurt or milk

½ cup real butter, melted

2 large cloves garlic, minced

1. Place warm water in a bowl and add sugar. Stir gently and sprinkle in yeast. Let stand 10 minutes or until bubbly.

2. While yeast is proofing, add 3 cups flour and the salt to a stand mixer fitted with the dough hook (or a large mixing bowl if you do not have a stand mixer). Add proofed yeast mixture, egg, and yogurt or milk. Mix until it forms a very soft dough; add additional flour if needed but keep dough very soft and sticky to the touch. Knead with dough hook for 5 minutes (or by hand if not using a stand mixer).

3. Place in a lightly oiled bowl in a warm location and cover with a light towel. Let rise until nearly double in size, about 45 minutes to 1 hour. Punch down dough onto a lightly floured surface. Form into a mound and divide into 12–14 equal-sized portions. Place portions on a baking sheet and let rise again about 30 minutes until double in size. While dough is rising, preheat grill, panini press, or skillet.

4. Place butter in a small bowl and add garlic.

5. When dough has risen and the pan is hot, lightly brush the pan with garlic butter. Roll out each portion of dough slightly thicker than a tortilla, about ⅛ inch. Place dough on hot pan and grill 1–3 minutes until small bubbles form on top. Brush top side with garlic butter and flip. Cook an additional 1–3 minutes until golden brown on each side. Transfer to a plate and cover with foil to keep warm while making the remaining flatbread. Serve as a side dish with hummus or the remaining garlic butter, or use as wraps for Gyro Burger Pitas (page 98) or fill with Grilled Tandoori-Style Chicken (page 94).

Tabbouleh

This Middle Eastern salad (pronounced tuh-BOO-luh) showcases all sorts of summer deliciousness such as tomatoes, cucumbers, and parsley. You'll find bulgur wheat in the health food section of the grocery store.

1 cup bulgur wheat

2 cups boiling water

2 tomatoes, seeded and diced

½ medium cucumber, diced

¼ cup sliced green onions

1 cup chopped fresh parsley

2 tablespoons chopped fresh mint, optional

¼ cup olive oil

1 tablespoon plus 1 teaspoon fresh lemon juice

1 teaspoon kosher salt

½ teaspoon freshly ground black pepper

¾ teaspoon ground cumin

Serves 8–10

🌱 **Vegetarian**

ROLLOVERS
Cucumber
Green onions
Parsley

TIP: This salad becomes more delicious over the course of a few days. It's a great, light main dish, but it also pairs well with grilled chicken or fish.

1. Place bulgur wheat in a medium-sized bowl and pour boiling water over it. Lightly stir and cover the bowl with plastic wrap. Set aside for 45 minutes without removing plastic. After 45 minutes, place bulgur in a fine-mesh strainer and press on it with a wooden spoon to remove any excess moisture.

2. Place bulgur wheat, tomatoes, cucumber, green onions, parsley, (and mint, if using) in a mixing bowl and toss lightly. Add oil, lemon juice, salt, pepper, and cumin. Gently toss until everything is well distributed. Cover bowl and refrigerate a minimum of 1 hour before serving and preferably for 2–4 hours. Toss before serving.

☆ **Make Ahead**

🌿 **Vegetarian**

ROLLOVER
Green onions

TIP: Pepitas are small pumpkin seeds. Look for bags of these roasted, nutty-flavored seeds near the sunflower seeds in the grocery store. If you can't find them, sunflower seeds are a good substitute.

MAKE-AHEAD

INSTRUCTIONS: To make ahead of time, prepare salad and dressing and reserve walnuts and pepitas. Store all ingredients separately in the refrigerator for up to 24 hours. Combine everything just before serving, or store fully prepared in the refrigerator for up to 1 hour.

Tropical Slaw with Pineapple Vinaigrette

Try this tropical-flavored slaw instead of the traditional creamy coleslaws. It's delicious with Grilled Coconut-Lime Skewers (page 90) or Thai Spring Rolls (page 91).

Salad

8 cups shredded coleslaw or sliced cabbage mix (about 1 small to medium head cabbage)

1 medium to large carrot, shredded

⅓ cup sliced green onions

½ cup dried cranberries

¾ cup diced dried mangoes

¼ cup roughly chopped walnuts, toasted

¼ cup pepitas (see Tip)

Dressing

¾ cup pineapple juice (one 6-ounce can)

3 tablespoons vegetable oil

1½ tablespoons cider vinegar

1 large clove garlic, pressed

½ teaspoon salt

⅛ teaspoon freshly ground black pepper

1 tablespoon sugar

1. **For the salad:** Place all salad ingredients in a salad bowl and place in the refrigerator to chill. If preparing salad in advance, reserve walnuts and pepitas and add them just before serving.

2. **For the dressing:** Place all ingredients in a screw-top jar and shake vigorously for 1 minute. Pour desired amount over salad (you may not need all of it) and toss to combine. Serve immediately or chill up to 1 hour before serving.

Makes 4 main dish servings
or 8 side dish servings

⊙ **Quick and Easy**

ROLLOVERS
Feta cheese
Parmesan cheese
Spinach

SERVING SUGGESTION:
The Berry-Poppy Seed Vinaigrette is
also delicious on baby spinach with
sliced red onions and candied nuts. Use
whatever berries (or combination of
berries) you happen to have on hand,
fresh or frozen.

Grilled Chicken and Berry Salad

This salad is a make-at-home version of one of our favorite take-out salads, only we love it even more! Use pre-grilled chicken for a super-fast, healthy lunch or dinner in the middle of the summer. For a vegetarian meal, omit the chicken.

½ head romaine lettuce, washed and chopped into bite-sized pieces

6–8 ounces baby spinach

12–16 ounces chicken (marinated, grilled, and sliced)

8 ounces strawberries, sliced

8 ounces blueberries

4 ounces crumbled feta or shredded fresh Parmesan cheese

1 cup sliced almonds, toasted

Berry-Poppy Seed Vinaigrette, to taste

For serving a large crowd, toss all the salad ingredients in a large serving bowl and add dressing, to taste. For individual servings, arrange ingredients on plates and serve dressing on the side.

Berry-Poppy Seed Vinaigrette (makes 2 cups)

½ cup white wine vinegar

½ cup honey (or sugar)

1–2 cloves garlic

1 tablespoon grated onion

1 teaspoon kosher or other coarse salt

About 10 cracks of freshly ground black pepper

1 cup raspberries, blackberries, or strawberries

⅔ cup canola oil

1½ teaspoons poppy seeds

Combine vinegar, honey, garlic, onion, salt, pepper, and berries in a blender and process until smooth. With the blender running on a lower speed, add the oil in a steady stream. Turn off the blender and whisk in the poppy seeds. If possible, refrigerate at least an hour before serving.

⊕ **Quick and Easy**

ROLLOVER
Parmesan cheese

TIP: For easy preparation, make dressing, croutons (if making your own), and chicken ahead of time and toss together just before serving.

VARIATION: Place some salad in a large tortilla and roll it up for a salad wrap.

Grilled Chicken Caesar Salad

It's not hard to throw together a Caesar salad with ready-made ingredients, but making one from scratch really brings this classic restaurant dish to your table. Fresh garlic, lemon juice, Parmesan cheese, high-quality mustard, and cracked black pepper make this at-home version so much better than anything from a bottle.

⅓ cup mayonnaise

1½ tablespoons Dijon mustard

3–4 garlic gloves, roughly chopped

3 tablespoons fresh lemon juice

½ tablespoon white wine vinegar

¼ teaspoon kosher salt

¼ teaspoon black pepper

1 cup pure or light olive oil (see Tip on page 16)

2–3 tablespoons milk, if needed

8 ounces boneless, skinless chicken breast (about 2 medium), butterflied

1–2 heads romaine lettuce (about 12 cups torn)

½ cup shredded fresh Parmesan cheese, plus more for garnish

1 batch Sourdough Garlic-Herb Croutons (page 87)

Lemon wedges, for garnish

1. Combine mayonnaise, mustard, garlic, lemon juice, vinegar, salt, and pepper in a blender and process until smooth. With blender running on low speed, slowly pour olive oil in a steady stream just until fully incorporated. Only if needed, add milk by the tablespoon until desired consistency is reached. Place ½ cup dressing in a zip-top bag with chicken breasts and marinate at least 30 minutes or as long as overnight. Place remaining dressing in refrigerator to chill.

2. Preheat grill to medium heat. Remove chicken breasts from marinade and let excess drip off. Grill chicken 4–5 minutes on each side until cooked through or internal temperature reaches 165 degrees F. Remove from grill and let rest at least 5 minutes before slicing. Let cool to room temperature and then store in refrigerator until ready to use. This step can be done ahead of time.

3. Wash lettuce and tear into bite-sized pieces. Place in bowl and toss with Parmesan cheese, croutons, and prepared chicken. Toss with dressing, to taste. Top each serving with additional Parmesan cheese, freshly cracked black pepper, and lemon wedges.

Greek Salad Dressing

This is one of our favorite newer recipes. Bottled dressings don't even begin to compare with how flavorful and fresh this is. And it's not just great for salads— try marinating chicken, beef, or lamb in this dressing overnight before grilling.

¼ cup freshly squeezed lemon juice

¼ cup white vinegar

2 teaspoons sugar

½ teaspoon kosher salt

½ teaspoon seasoning salt

½ teaspoon red pepper flakes (this will not make the dressing spicy, just flavorful)

¼ teaspoon freshly ground black pepper

4 cloves garlic, smashed and peeled

1 cup canola oil (or other salad oil)

½ cup crumbled feta cheese

¾ teaspoon Italian seasoning

¼ teaspoon dried oregano

Combine lemon juice, vinegar, sugar, salt, seasoning salt, red pepper flakes, pepper, and garlic in a blender and process until smooth. While the blender is running, add the oil in a steady stream. Turn off the blender, add the feta, and pulse a few times (more if you want a creamier consistency). Whisk in Italian seasoning and oregano. Refrigerate at least 1 hour before serving, if possible.

Sourdough Garlic-Herb Croutons

These sourdough croutons are the best part of any Texas-style steakhouse green salad and are perfect on any tossed green salad at home, but they're also delicious on top of soups such as our Split Pea Soup with Ham (page 23). That is, of course, if you can stop snacking on them first.

Makes 4 cups of croutons

ROLLOVER
Parmesan cheese

¼ teaspoon kosher salt

¼ teaspoon onion powder

½ teaspoon granulated garlic

½ teaspoon dried oregano

1 teaspoon dried parsley

1 tablespoon real butter

1½ tablespoons extra virgin olive oil

4 cups sourdough bread cubes

1–2 tablespoons crumbled Parmesan cheese, optional, but recommended

1. Preheat oven to 350 degrees F.

2. Combine salt, onion powder, garlic, oregano, and parsley in a small bowl. Set aside.

3. Melt butter in the microwave until completely melted and then combine it with oil. Place bread cubes in a large bowl and drizzle butter and oil mixture over the bread cubes evenly.

4. Toss the cubes with your hands to make sure each cube is coated with the butter mixture. Distribute the herb mixture evenly over the bread cubes, and toss again with your hands.

5. Spread cubes in a single layer on a baking sheet. Place in oven and bake 8–10 minutes. Use a spatula to flip and stir croutons and then bake an additional 5–10 minutes or until golden brown and toasted.

6. When finished, remove from oven and immediately toss with Parmesan cheese, if desired. Let cool completely. Store in an airtight container.

Serves 4–6

ROLLOVERS
Parsley
Red onion

TIP 1: Not all ground turkey is created equal. While ground turkey breast can be almost completely fat-free, some ground turkey can have just as much if not more fat than regular ground beef. If you're eating turkey for health reasons, be sure to check the nutritional information on the packaging.

TIP 2: Because most ground turkey is so lean, it has a tendency to shrink while cooking, so you might wind up with turkey golf balls instead of burgers. After you form the patties, make a ½-inch-deep indentation with your thumb and your burgers will stay patty-shaped.

Peach Mayo Spread

½ cup mayonnaise

¼ cup peach preserves

1 teaspoon mild Dijon or coarsely ground mustard

Whisk all ingredients together.

Peach-Kissed Turkey Burgers

Light and healthy, these turkey burgers have a hint of sweetness from summery peaches and are great for warm summer nights.

1½ tablespoons olive oil

⅓ cup minced onion

3 cloves garlic, finely minced

20 ounces (1¼ pounds) ground turkey breast (see Tips 1 and 2)

2 tablespoons fresh minced parsley or 2 teaspoons dry parsley

1½ teaspoons kosher salt

½ teaspoon freshly ground black pepper

¼ cup peach jam

1 teaspoon Dijon or coarsely ground mustard

1½ teaspoons Worcestershire sauce

4–6 quality buns or rolls

Lettuce

Red onion slices

Tomatoes

1. Heat oil in a small nonstick skillet over medium heat. Add onion and garlic and sauté, stirring frequently to prevent burning, for 2–3 minutes or until onion is tender and garlic is fragrant. Remove pan from heat and set aside.

2. Place ground turkey in a mixing bowl and break up with a fork. Add parsley, salt, pepper, peach jam, mustard, and Worcestershire sauce. Add sautéed onion and garlic and all oil left in pan. *Important note:* Do not discard the olive oil. Adding it to the meat improves the burgers' texture and keeps them moist. Use a fork to gently toss the meat to distribute ingredients evenly. To keep meat tender, do not overwork.

3. Divide meat into 4 large patties or 6 smaller patties, forming evenly sized balls and then gently shaping into patties. Burgers can be made up to this point and then frozen or stored in the refrigerator up to 24 hours before cooking. For best results, chill patties at least 1 hour before cooking.

4. Preheat indoor grill pan, skillet on the stove top, or outdoor grill to medium-high heat. Brush hot cooking surface with vegetable oil. Place patties on cooking surface and cook 5–7 minutes on each side (flip only once), or until internal temperature reaches 165 degrees F.

5. Spread toasted buns with Peach Mayo Spread. Add cooked patties, lettuce, onion slices, and tomatoes and serve immediately.

ROLLOVERS
Cilantro
Coconut milk
Ginger

Grilled Coconut-Lime Skewers

You can use fresh shelled shrimp, chicken thighs, or flank steak in this sweet, spicy, tangy marinade. Use the leftovers in Thai Spring Rolls (see facing page).

1 (12-ounce) can Coca-Cola

3 cloves garlic, minced or pressed

1 teaspoon minced ginger

¼ cup soy sauce

½ teaspoon Sriracha sauce

1 tablespoon ketchup

⅓ cup coconut milk

Juice of 2 limes

2 tablespoons dark brown sugar

1½ pounds boneless, skinless chicken thighs, shelled shrimp, or flank steak, cut into bite-sized pieces

1. Combine all ingredients, except meat, in a small saucepan and bring to a boil. Remove from heat and cool to room temperature.

2. Place the meat in a large zip-top bag and pour the cooled marinade over it. Refrigerate at least 4 hours. When ready to cook, thread the meat onto skewers and grill 3–4 minutes per side or until desired doneness is reached. Serve with Peanut Dipping Sauce.

Peanut Dipping Sauce

Nonstick cooking spray or 1 teaspoon olive oil

1 teaspoon freshly minced garlic (about 1 clove)

1 teaspoon minced ginger

¼ cup soy sauce

¼ cup brown sugar

¼ cup creamy peanut butter

¼ teaspoon Thai curry paste

½ cup coconut milk

Heat oil over medium heat in a small saucepan. Add garlic and ginger and sauté 1–2 minutes or until fragrant and tender. Add remaining ingredients and heat, stirring constantly, until warm and smooth. Remove from heat and serve with Grilled Coconut-Lime Skewers, your favorite grilled meats, or Thai Spring Rolls.

Thai Spring Rolls

Use the leftovers from the Grilled Coconut-Lime Skewers (see facing page) to avoid heating up your kitchen in the summer.

12 rice paper wraps (available in the Asian foods section of a grocery store or specialty store)

1½ cups Mango Rice (page 118)

Leftover meat from Grilled Coconut-Lime Skewers (see facing page)

½ medium cucumber, julienned

½ red bell pepper, julienned

1 medium carrot, julienned

1 cup loosely packed bean sprouts

Chopped cilantro and/or mint

1. Soak rice papers according to package directions.

2. To assemble the rolls, place 1½ to 2 tablespoons Mango Rice on each wrapper. Top with desired toppings, wrap, and serve with Peanut Dipping Sauce (see facing page).

Makes 12 rolls

ROLLOVERS
Bell pepper
Cucumber

Grilled Summer Vegetable Sandwich

These sandwiches on thick artisan bread highlight summer's heartiest vegetables. Bursting with color and flavor, they're great for lunch parties as a main dish or sliced into small pieces for an appetizer. Serve with fresh fruit and hand-squeezed lemonade for a filling summer meal.

Makes 6–8 large sandwiches or 12–16 party sandwiches

🌿 **Vegetarian**

ROLLOVER
Basil

❈ *Author's Note*

This is one of my favorite things to serve at parties, especially baby and wedding showers. It can be prepped ahead of time and then sliced into small pieces to serve a crowd. Plus, it looks gorgeous! It's always nice to have something filling for those who don't eat meat, but you can also slip some thin slices of salami in there for an extra burst of flavor.
—Sara

⅔ cup mayonnaise

Zest from 1 medium lemon

2 teaspoons fresh lemon juice

1 garlic clove, pressed (about 1 teaspoon)

1 yellow squash

1 medium zucchini

1 medium eggplant

1 medium red or sweet yellow onion

Olive oil for brushing

Kosher salt

Freshly ground black pepper

1 (12-ounce) loaf focaccia bread

8 ounces sliced mozzarella or provolone cheese

1 (6-ounce) jar roasted red peppers (drained), or 2–3 tomatoes, sliced

1 cup loosely packed basil leaves

1. Stir together mayonnaise, lemon zest, lemon juice, and garlic. Place in an airtight container in the refrigerator until ready to use. Can be prepared a day ahead of time.

2. Preheat outdoor grill or indoor grill pan to about 400 degrees F. Line a large baking sheet with foil. Slice squash and zucchini into ¼-inch slices on a slight diagonal. Slice eggplant and onion into ¼-inch slices. Place sliced vegetables on baking sheet in a single layer and brush lightly with oil. Sprinkle lightly with salt and pepper. Grill vegetables in batches, 3–4 minutes on each side, or until tender and showing grill marks.

3. While vegetables are grilling, slice the entire focaccia loaf in half horizontally and spread lemon-garlic mayonnaise on each side. Layer sliced cheese on each side of bread. As warm veggies come off the grill, place them directly on the bottom half of the focaccia. Top with roasted red peppers or tomatoes and basil leaves. If desired, place top half of focaccia under broiler to melt the cheese and then place on top of sandwich. Serve warm or at room temperature.

ROLLOVER
Greek yogurt

Indian Rice

2 teaspoons olive oil

¼ cup diced onion

2 cups water

2 chicken bouillon cubes

1 teaspoon ground turmeric

½ teaspoon curry powder

1 cup jasmine rice

Heat medium-sized pot to medium heat on stove top. Add oil and onion and cook until onion is tender, about 3 minutes. Add water and bouillon cubes and increase heat until water boils. Use a spoon to break up bouillon cubes. Add turmeric, curry powder, and rice and stir to combine. Reduce heat to low simmer, cover, and cook 20 minutes or until all water is absorbed. Fluff with fork before serving.

Grilled Tandoori-Style Chicken

This is our take on a classic Indian dish. Yogurt helps keep the chicken moist and flavorful, and using chicken thighs adds a lot of flavor. Serve it with Indian Rice (at left) and Naan (page 76) or pita bread.

8–10 boneless, skinless chicken thighs (about 2½ pounds)

¾ cup plain Greek yogurt

1 lemon, zested and then juiced

4 cloves garlic, roughly chopped

⅓ cup chopped white onion

¼ cup extra virgin olive oil

1½ teaspoons kosher salt

¼ teaspoon freshly ground black pepper

1 tablespoon paprika

2 teaspoons ground cumin

2 teaspoons ground ginger

1 teaspoon turmeric

½ teaspoon ground red pepper (less if you want the chicken less spicy)

Cilantro, for garnish, optional

1. Rinse chicken thighs in cold water and pat dry. Trim off excess fat, if necessary, and place chicken in a large, heavy-duty zip-top bag.

2. Place all remaining ingredients, except cilantro, in a blender or food processor. Process until smooth and then pour into bag with chicken. Toss to coat all chicken pieces. Place in refrigerator and marinate a minimum of 8 hours and preferably 24 hours.

3. Preheat grill to medium-high heat. Lightly oil grill grates to avoid sticking. Remove chicken pieces from bag and allow excess marinade to drip off. Place chicken on grill and close lid. Cook 4–6 minutes before flipping chicken pieces over and then cook an additional 4–6 minutes on the other side or until chicken reaches an internal temperature of 165 degrees F.

Chicken can also be cooked on a broiler pan or indoor grill pan.

⊕ **Quick and Easy**

ROLLOVERS
Cilantro
Red onion

Sweet Chili Chicken with Pineapple Salsa

Using chicken tenders makes this recipe super quick and easy. Look for sweet chili sauce in the Asian foods section of a well-stocked grocery store—Thai Kitchen is a popular brand found in most locations.

Juice from 1 large lime (2–3 tablespoons)

1½ teaspoons curry powder

2 teaspoons vegetable or olive oil

1 pound chicken tenders (about 8 tenders)

Kosher salt and black pepper, for light sprinkling

Lime wedges, optional, for garnish

Salsa

1½ cups diced pineapple

⅓ cup thinly sliced red onion

1 avocado, diced

1 tablespoon fresh lime juice

3 tablespoons chopped cilantro

Pinch of kosher salt

Sauce

3 tablespoons sweet chili sauce

1 tablespoon honey

1½ teaspoons soy sauce

1 tablespoon warm water

1. Place lime juice, curry powder, and oil in a large zip-top bag and shake lightly to combine. Add chicken tenders and marinate at least 30 minutes, and up to 4 hours. Preheat grill or indoor grill pan to medium-high heat and lightly oil grill grates. Remove chicken from marinade and sprinkle both sides lightly with salt and pepper. Grill chicken about 3 minutes on each side, or until internal temperature registers 165 degrees F.

2. **For the salsa:** Combine all salsa ingredients and gently toss to combine. Refrigerate until ready to use.

3. **For the sauce:** Combine sweet chili sauce, honey, soy sauce, and warm water and whisk with a fork until smooth.

4. To serve, plate grilled chicken tenders, top with salsa, and drizzle with sauce. Serve with lime wedges, if desired.

⊙ **Quick and Easy**

ROLLOVERS
Cucumber
Greek yogurt
Green onions
Rosemary

Gyro Burger Pitas

If you love gyros at your favorite Greek restaurant, try these Greek-seasoned lamb burgers topped with cool, creamy Tzatziki and folded into a pita.

1 pound lean ground lamb (if this is hard to find, ask a butcher to grind 1 pound of lamb leg or loin; you can also use lean ground beef)

4 cloves garlic, minced

1½ teaspoons dried minced onion

1 tablespoon Dijon or Creole mustard

¾ teaspoon kosher salt

¼ teaspoon freshly ground black pepper

1 tablespoon red wine vinegar

½ teaspoon dried oregano

1 teaspoon chopped rosemary, dried or fresh

4 whole wheat pitas or 6-inch rounds of flatbread

Thin onion slices

Fresh tomato slices

Tzatziki

1. Gently combine lamb, garlic, onion, mustard, salt, pepper, vinegar, oregano, and rosemary with your hands and shape into 4 oblong patties (they'll fit better in the pitas). Grill 5–6 minutes on each side and remove from heat.

2. Allow to stand 5 minutes. Place on pitas or flatbread and add onion, tomatoes, and Tzatziki. Fold like a taco and serve immediately. For easy serving and cleanup, wrap in aluminum foil.

Tzatziki

1½ cups plain Greek yogurt

1 clove garlic, minced

1–2 teaspoons lemon juice

3 green onions, white ends finely chopped

1 teaspoon dried dill weed

½ medium cucumber, peeled, seeded, and thinly sliced

Kosher salt and freshly ground black pepper, to taste

Combine ingredients in a small bowl and season with salt and pepper, to taste. Store covered in refrigerator up to 3 days.

Serves 4–6

♥ Family Favorite

☺ Quick and Easy

ROLLOVER
Sour Cream

Tartar Sauce

½ cup mayonnaise

2 tablespoons sour cream

¼ teaspoon dried dill

½ teaspoon dried parsley

1½ teaspoons finely minced onion

1 tablespoon minced dill pickle

1 pinch seasoned salt

1 teaspoon fresh lemon juice

Mix all ingredients in a small bowl and stir well to combine. Chill at least 1 hour before serving (the longer the better; make ahead if you can!).

Baked Fish Sticks with Tartar Sauce

Unlike frozen fish sticks, these pieces of tender white fish are hand-seasoned and baked, so you don't have to feel guilty about serving these for a fast meal. The tartar sauce is awesome, but if you want to mix things up a little, try the Dipping Sauce on page 110.

1 tablespoon canola oil

1–2 eggs

¼ cup plus 2 tablespoons all-purpose flour

1 teaspoon seasoned salt

½ teaspoon freshly ground black pepper

½ teaspoon paprika

½ cup panko bread crumbs

½ cup unseasoned bread crumbs

1 pound white fish such as cod, halibut, or tilapia

1. Preheat oven to 450 degrees F. Line a baking sheet with aluminum foil and brush oil over the foil. Set aside.

2. Beat egg lightly in a shallow dish (use another egg later if you need to). Combine flour, seasoned salt, pepper, and paprika in a separate shallow dish. Set aside. Combine panko and regular bread crumbs in a third shallow dish. Set aside.

3. Cut fish into sticks 3–4 inches long and ½–1-inch wide.

4. Working with a few pieces of fish at a time, dredge fish first in flour and then shake off excess. Then dip each piece in beaten egg and then in the bread crumb mixture. Make sure all sides are well coated with bread crumbs and then place fish on the baking sheet.

5. When all pieces are on the baking sheet, place in oven and bake about 10 minutes. Cool a few minutes and then serve with Tartar Sauce for dipping.

How to Grill the Perfect Steak

Making a steak at home can be intimidating, but we're here to help make sure your steaks come out delicious, juicy, and cooked to perfection every time! Follow these steps and you'll be on your way to steak night at home instead of at a pricey restaurant.

1. Choose a good cut of meat. For grilling, we love rib eyes and New York strip. T-bone and porterhouse are both premium cuts. Tri-tip is another great one.

2. Let steaks sit at room temperature about 10–15 minutes while your grill is preheating. Trim excess fat from around edges of steaks, but don't remove all fat. Season both sides of steaks liberally with kosher salt and freshly cracked pepper.

3. Heat your grill to high heat. If using charcoal, move heated coals to one side of the grill so you have both direct and indirect heat.

4. Lightly oil grill if needed. Use a pair of tongs to hold a paper towel dipped in oil, or use tongs to hold a piece of the trimmed fat to quickly and lightly grease grill grates.

5. Sear. Place steaks on hot grill and do not move for about 2–3 minutes. If diamond grill marks are desired, rotate meat 45 degrees and grill a little longer. Use tongs (not a fork) to flip steaks and cook 2–3 more minutes.

6. Finish cooking. Turn heat down to medium-high and close grill lid if you have one. If using charcoal, move steaks to the side not directly above coals. Continue to cook until internal temperature reaches temperatures shown below. Keep in mind that most cuts of steak will have the best flavor and texture if cooked to medium or rarer.

> **Rare:** 120–125 degrees F.
>
> **Medium-Rare:** 130–135 degrees F.
>
> **Medium:** 140–145 degrees F.
>
> **Medium-Well:** 150–155 degrees F.
>
> **Well Done:** 160 degrees F. +

7. Rest. Use tongs to remove steaks from grill and cover steaks with foil to keep warm. Let rest at least 5 minutes before cutting to let the juices redistribute.

8. Enjoy!

Hand Test for Steak Doneness

Although internal temperature readings are the most accurate way to test steak doneness, our "hand test" works great as a gauge. (See photos below.) Hold your non-dominant hand with fingers extended and using the index finger on your opposite hand, gently press the lower palm near the bottom of the thumb as shown in Figure 1. This is similar to pressing on the top center of a rare steak. While still pressing the same spot, touch your thumb and pointer finger together as shown in Figure 2. Notice how the muscle feels firmer; this is similar to pressing on a medium-rare steak. Continue following the images below to get a feel for meat doneness. With a little practice, you will be able to tell how done a steak is by gently pressing on the top of it.

RARE

Figure 1

MEDIUM-RARE

Figure 2

MEDIUM

MEDIUM-WELL   **WELL DONE**

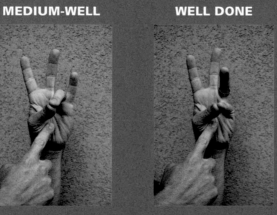

TIP: For an easy gift for dads who love to grill, fill empty spice bottles with this rub and include it with a package of nice steaks.

All-Purpose Meat and Veggie Rub

Dads and grill-lovers will love this mix of herbs and spices. This rub is delicious mixed into burgers, rubbed onto steaks or ribs, or whisked into oil and drizzled over whole mushrooms before grilling.

2 teaspoons dried oregano

2 teaspoons kosher salt

1 teaspoon coarse, freshly ground black pepper

1 tablespoon granulated garlic

1 tablespoon onion powder

1 tablespoon brown sugar

2 teaspoons smoked paprika

Combine ingredients and mix until well distributed.

For burgers: Mix 1 tablespoon rub, 1½ tablespoons coarse-grained or Creole (such as Zatarain's) mustard, and 1 pound 85 percent lean ground beef. Shape into patties and grill until desired doneness is reached.

For steak and chicken: Rub 1–1½ tablespoons into 16 ounces of steak or chicken pieces and allow to stand about 10 minutes before grilling.

For vegetables: Lightly brush vegetables with olive or vegetable oil and sprinkle with rub. Grill a few minutes on each side until grill marks appear and vegetables are crisp-tender.

♥ **Family Favorite**

TIPS: The Garlicky Blue Cheese Spread and Spiced Barbecue Sauce can both be made 2–3 days ahead of time, which helps reduce actual meal preparation time.

Garlicky Blue Cheese Spread

½ cup mayonnaise

¼ teaspoon kosher salt

¼ teaspoon freshly ground black pepper

1 tablespoon red wine vinegar

1 clove garlic, pressed or finely minced

¼ cup crumbled blue cheese (you can use feta if you don't love blue cheese)

Whisk together mayonnaise, salt, pepper, red wine vinegar, and garlic. Stir in crumbled blue cheese. Store in refrigerator until ready to use.

Barbecue Bacon Sliders with Crispy Shoestring Onions

This was the recipe we used to win the Better Homes and Gardens *cook-off in 2010, and it never disappoints! Juicy, seasoned ground beef on a soft bun with a leaf of cool lettuce, crisp bacon, garlicky blue cheese mayonnaise, and crunchy fried onions? Yeah, you can't go wrong there.*

1½ pounds high-quality 85% lean ground beef

½ cup Spiced Barbecue Sauce (page 109) or your favorite bottled barbecue sauce, divided

½ teaspoon kosher salt

¼ teaspoon freshly ground black pepper

8–10 small white dinner rolls or sweet Hawaiian rolls, sliced in half, and toasted, if desired

Garlicky Blue Cheese Spread (at left)

8–10 crisp lettuce leaves

8–10 slices bacon, cooked crisp

Crispy Shoestring Onions (page 108)

1. Heat a grill pan on the stove top or outdoor grill to medium-high heat. Combine beef, 2 tablespoons barbecue sauce, salt, and pepper. Divide and shape mixture into 8–10 ¾-inch-thick patties. (When shaping the patties, keep the size of your bun in mind, as well as the fact that the burgers will shrink quite a bit while cooking.)

2. Grill 2–3 minutes and then flip. Brush the top side of each burger with some of remaining sauce. Continue grilling another 2 minutes and flip burgers again, brushing the other side with additional sauce. Continue to cook and brush with more sauce until internal temperature of the burgers reaches 160–165 degrees F.

3. To assemble, lightly spread the bottom half of each bun with Garlicky Blue Cheese Spread and top with a lettuce leaf. Break each bacon piece in half and place on top of lettuce leaves. Place burger on top and drizzle with additional barbecue sauce, if desired. Top with a small handful of Crispy Shoestring Onions. Spread remaining Garlicky Blue Cheese Spread on top halves of buns.

TIP: This recipe makes a lot, so make only half if you don't think you'll use them all.

Crispy Shoestring Onions

These little fried gems of deliciousness are the crowning glory of our Barbecue Bacon Sliders (page 106) and Homemade Green Bean Casserole (page 164), but they're also a fabulous little snack. Just be sure to have people to share them with because before you know it, they'll all be gone.

Vegetable oil for frying

1 large white or yellow onion, cut in half and then thinly sliced

2 eggs

2 tablespoons milk or buttermilk

1½ cups flour

2 teaspoons salt

2 teaspoons black pepper

2 teaspoons garlic powder

1. Heat at least 2 inches of oil to 350 degrees F. Make sure to use a pot with high sides (as opposed to a skillet-style pan) so oil doesn't boil over when you add the onion.

2. Whisk eggs and milk together in a medium-sized bowl with a fork. Combine flour, salt, pepper, and garlic powder in a separate bowl.

3. Working with a handful of onion slices at a time, dip them in egg mixture and let excess drip off. Then dredge in flour mixture and toss lightly to coat. Place slices in hot oil, being careful not to crowd the pan, and cook until golden brown. Remove with slotted spoon and place on folded paper towels to absorb excess oil. Repeat process until all onions are fried. Serve with Dipping Sauce (page 110), or whip up an easy dip by whisking 1 part barbecue sauce and 1 part mayonnaise.

Spiced Barbecue Sauce

Don't be scared of the long list of ingredients—almost everything is probably already in your refrigerator or pantry! This sweet and spicy barbecue sauce is an amazing addition to grilled chicken, ribs, or brisket. Try it on our award-winning Barbecue Bacon Sliders (page 106) with Crispy Shoestring Onions (see facing page).

1 tablespoon olive oil

½ cup finely chopped onion

2 cloves garlic, minced

¾ cup apple juice

1 (6-ounce) can tomato paste

¼ cup cider vinegar

2 tablespoons packed dark brown sugar, plus more to taste, if desired

2 tablespoons molasses

1 teaspoon yellow mustard

1 tablespoon paprika (use smoked paprika if you prefer a smoky sauce)

1 pinch cinnamon

1 pinch cloves

1 pinch cayenne pepper

1 tablespoon Worcestershire sauce

1 teaspoon kosher salt

½ teaspoon freshly ground black pepper

1 tablespoon prepared horseradish (see Tip 1)

Heat oil over medium heat in a medium saucepan. Add onion and garlic, stirring frequently, until onion is translucent. Add remaining ingredients, except horseradish, and bring to a simmer, stirring frequently. Taste and add additional sugar if a sweeter sauce is desired. Turn heat to low, cover, and cook for 30 minutes, stirring frequently. Add horseradish and serve.

Makes about 2 cups

TIP 1: Horseradish loses its flavor and zing if it's cooked, so add it only when you're done simmering the sauce. Also, this sauce needs to be cooked at a low temperature and stirred frequently because if it burns, it will become very bitter.

TIP 2: Place the sauce in jars and deliver it to friends and neighbors as a gift or bring it to a potluck as a hostess gift.

ROLLOVERS
Buttermilk
Red onion
Spinach

Fried Green Tomatoes with Dipping Sauce

Canola oil for frying

3 medium to large firm green tomatoes

Kosher salt

Freshly cracked black pepper

½ cup all-purpose flour

1 large egg

½ cup buttermilk or milk

½ cup dry bread crumbs

½ cup cornmeal

1. Heat a medium-sized skillet with ½-inch oil to 350 degrees F.

2. Slice off top of tomatoes where stem is attached and discard. Continue slicing into ¼- to ½-inch slices and discard remaining end. Each tomato normally yields 3–5 slices. Place slices in a single layer on a cutting board or piece of foil. Sprinkle both sides lightly with salt and pepper.

3. Place flour in a shallow dish and set aside. Whisk together the egg and buttermilk in a separate shallow dish and set aside. Combine bread crumbs and cornmeal in a third shallow dish and set aside.

4. Lightly dredge each tomato slice in flour. Then dip both sides and edges in egg mixture and let excess drip off. Finally, dredge in bread crumb mixture. Place a few tomato slices in hot oil and fry until golden brown on each side, flipping once. Remove from oil and place on paper towels. Serve with Dipping Sauce.

Dipping Sauce

½ cup mayonnaise (not Miracle Whip)

1 tablespoon chopped capers

1 clove garlic, pressed or very finely minced

1½ teaspoons minced red onion

2 teaspoons fresh lime or lemon juice

2 teaspoons Creole or other mild coarse-grained mustard

⅛ teaspoon cayenne pepper

Pinch kosher salt

Whisk together the sauce ingredients and serve with Fried Green Tomatoes, French fries, or Baked Fish Sticks (page 100).

Fried Green Tomato BLT

2 slices rustic sandwich bread, toasted   2 slices bacon, cooked crisp

Dipping Sauce   2–3 slices Fried Green Tomatoes

Lettuce, spinach, or mixed greens

Spread each slice of toast with Dipping Sauce. Place greens on 1 slice of toast and top with bacon and Fried Green Tomato slices. Top with remaining slice of toast.

ROLLOVER
Parmesan cheese

Baked Zucchini Fries

We can't guarantee that your kids and veggie-haters will love this, but if you're going to get them to eat zucchini, this might be the only way! These zucchini fries are a great alternative to French fries and are a delicious accompaniment to Italian-style meals.

¼ cup all-purpose flour

½ cup Italian-seasoned panko bread crumbs

¼ cup grated Parmesan cheese (the crumbly type, not shreds)

2 eggs

1 pound zucchini

1. Preheat oven to 425 degrees F. Line a baking sheet with aluminum foil and spray with nonstick cooking spray. Set aside.

2. Place flour in a shallow bowl and set aside. Combine bread crumbs and Parmesan cheese in a separate bowl and set aside. Whisk 2 eggs together in a shallow pie plate and set aside.

3. Cut the ends off the zucchini and then cut zucchini in half crosswise so you have two short, stubby pieces. Set one piece on its end and cut it in half lengthwise. Cut that half in half, making 2 planks. Repeat with the remaining halves (8 planks per zucchini).

4. Stack 2 planks on top of each other and cut into strips. Thicker strips will yield "meatier" fries with more zucchini flavor, while thin strips will be crispy and taste virtually nothing like zucchini. When all the fries are cut, blot pieces with a paper towel.

5. Working with a small handful of strips at a time, dredge zucchini in flour and shake to remove any excess. Dip in egg, shake to remove any excess, and then roll in about 2–3 tablespoons of bread crumbs at a time, adding more as needed. Don't work with all the bread crumbs at once because they'll soak up moisture from the egg and won't stick to the zucchini. Place coated strips on the prepared baking sheet and repeat until all the zucchini strips have been coated.

6. Bake 10–12 minutes. Remove from oven, flip the fries, and bake another 10–12 minutes or until zucchini is not soggy and the coating is crisp and golden brown. Serve with warmed bottled spaghetti sauce, your favorite Ranch dressing, or your favorite pizza sauce.

Fresh Tomato-Basil Pasta

Fresh tomatoes and basil are simmered and then served over delicate angel hair pasta for a light dinner using the bounty from your garden (or the produce department—we don't discriminate). Top with freshly grated Parmesan cheese and serve with a side of crusty bread and a tossed green salad.

¼ cup extra virgin olive oil

⅓ cup finely diced onion

5–6 cloves garlic, pressed or minced

3 pounds fresh tomatoes, diced with juices (about 6 cups)

1 teaspoon kosher salt

¼ teaspoon coarse, freshly ground black pepper

2 tablespoons balsamic vinegar

1 teaspoon sugar

½ cup chopped fresh basil

½ pound angel hair pasta, cooked according to package instructions

½ cup freshly grated Parmesan cheese, plus more if desired

1. Heat a large skillet to medium heat. When hot, add oil to coat pan. Add onion and garlic and sauté, stirring frequently, until onion is tender (about 4–6 minutes).

2. Add tomatoes, salt, pepper, vinegar, and sugar. Stir gently, breaking up tomatoes with the back of a spoon until they release some juices and come to a simmer. Simmer 30–45 minutes, stirring occasionally, until slightly thickened. Sauce will thicken the longer it is cooked.

3. Remove from heat and stir in basil. Toss with angel hair pasta and top with Parmesan cheese.

❋ Author's Note

After waiting patiently for my garden tomatoes to ripen, they often turn red all at once, and I find myself needing to use large quantities of tomatoes at a time! I mix and match all different types of tomatoes in this recipe, depending on what I have on hand or what's on sale at the store: Romas, Beefsteaks, and even tiny cherry tomatoes (my children's favorite) because they add extra sweetness. —*Sara*

Honey-Ginger Green Beans

Green beans are one of our all-time favorite summer veggies! These sweet and savory green beans will make everyone at your dinner table happy. They are perfect alongside Grilled Coconut-Lime Skewers (page 90).

1 pound fresh green beans, ends trimmed

½ teaspoon sesame oil

1 tablespoon honey

1 teaspoon cider vinegar

¼ teaspoon kosher salt

⅛ teaspoon freshly ground black pepper

1 tablespoon vegetable oil

1 tablespoon finely minced ginger

2 cloves garlic, pressed or finely minced

1 teaspoon toasted sesame seeds

1. Bring a large pot of salted water to a boil. Add green beans and cook 5–7 minutes, until crisp-tender.

2. While beans are cooking, combine sesame oil, honey, vinegar, salt, and pepper in a small bowl and set aside. Fill a large bowl half-full with ice water and set aside.

3. Remove beans from boiling water with a slotted spoon or mesh kitchen spider and plunge into the bowl of ice water to stop the cooking process and preserve the vibrant color. When cool, remove from ice bath and pat dry on paper towels.

4. Empty the pan you used to cook the beans and return it to the stove top on medium heat. Add oil and heat until oil is thin and shimmery. Add ginger and garlic and sauté about 1 minute or until tender and fragrant. Add drained beans and honey mixture and toss to combine. Stir until beans are heated through. Toss with sesame seeds and serve immediately, scraping the pan to include all the sauce and garlic.

Caramelized Onions

If you love to smother your steak with caramelized onions at a steakhouse, now you can do it at home! These are also delicious on burgers, sandwiches, pork (try the Apple Butter Pork Chops on page 152), wraps, and with potatoes.

½ tablespoon olive oil

½ tablespoon butter

2 large sweet onions, halved and thinly sliced

¼ teaspoon kosher salt

Black pepper, optional

½–1 teaspoon brown or white sugar, optional

Heat oil and butter in a large skillet over medium-high heat. When butter is melted, add onions. Toss with a spatula until onions are coated in oil and butter mixture. Reduce heat to medium/medium low and stir frequently about 10 minutes. Sprinkle with salt and continue to cook, stirring every few minutes, another 15–30 minutes or until onions are a rich amber color. If desired, add sugar about halfway through cooking process to enhance sweetness. Can be made up to 3 days ahead of time and stored in the refrigerator.

Makes 4 (¼-cup) servings

☆ **Make Ahead**

🌿 **Vegetarian**

OVEN INSTRUCTIONS:

For large amounts of onions, it's easier to cook them in the oven. To double the recipe, preheat oven to 400 degrees F. Place sliced onions in a large Dutch oven with a tight-fitting lid. Toss with oil, butter, salt, and pepper. Cover pan and cook 20 minutes. Remove pan to stir onions and add an additional tablespoon butter. Return pan to oven. Reduce heat to 350 degrees F. and cook another 40–50 minutes, stirring every 15–20 minutes, until onions are dark and caramelized.

⊕ **Quick and Easy**

🌿 **Vegetarian**

ROLLOVERS
Cilantro
Coconut milk
Green onions
Parsley

TIP: If you have problems with mushy rice, especially at low elevations, reduce water by 2 tablespoons.

Mango Rice

This sweet and savory rice is the perfect side for any dish with Asian or Latin flair. Look for coconut milk near the soy and almond milk in the dairy section—it's a better price than in individual cans and you can drink the delicious leftovers!

2 cups white or jasmine rice	2–3 teaspoons sugar
2 cups coconut milk	1 tablespoon butter
2 cups water	2 cups diced mango (2 medium mangoes)
1 teaspoon kosher salt	¼ cup chopped parsley or cilantro
1 teaspoon white vinegar (optional, but it helps with the texture)	½ cup sliced green onions
	¼ teaspoon black pepper

1. Combine rice, coconut milk, water, salt, vinegar, and sugar in a saucepan and bring to a boil. Turn heat to low and cook covered 20 minutes or until most of the liquid is absorbed. Allow to stand 5 minutes.

2. Add butter, mango, parsley or cilantro, green onions, black pepper, and additional salt, to taste.

Mascarpone Ice Cream with Balsamic Strawberry Sauce

Mascarpone (Italian cream cheese) makes this simple ice cream ultra creamy and flavorful. Don't be afraid to put vinegar into this recipe. Balsamic vinegar is commonly used in Italian desserts as it enhances both the natural flavor and color of sweet strawberries.

Ice Cream

1 cup whole milk

8 ounces mascarpone cheese

¾ cup sugar

1½ teaspoons vanilla extract

1 teaspoon almond extract

2 cups cream (not heavy cream)

Balsamic Strawberry Sauce

2 pints fresh strawberries, roughly chopped

½ cup sugar

3 tablespoons balsamic vinegar

Makes 8–10 (½-cup) servings

ROLLOVERS
Cream
Cream cheese (see Variation)

VARIATION: For an American twist, substitute regular cream cheese for mascarpone and garnish with some crushed graham crackers.

1. **For the ice cream:** Combine milk, mascarpone, sugar, vanilla, and almond extract in a blender. Process on low speed until combined and smooth and then continue blending about 30 seconds. Pour into an airtight, freezer-safe container and whisk in cream by hand. Freeze in ice cream maker according to manufacturer's directions and then transfer mixture back into freezer-safe container. Freeze until firm, about 3–4 hours.

2. **For the sauce:** Roughly chop berries and place in a small pan on medium heat. Add sugar and balsamic vinegar and stir to combine. As mixture heats, mash berries with the back of a spoon to release moisture. Bring sauce to a low simmer and continue to cook, stirring often, 20–25 minutes until thickened. Cool to room temperature and store in refrigerator until ready to use. Scoop ice cream into serving dishes and top with strawberry sauce.

ROLLOVER
Cream

TIP: This makes enough creamy topping for a very large pizza. Use extra topping as a delicious fruit dip or make two smaller pizzas.

Fruit Pizza

This updated version of the baby shower classic can be adapted depending on what fruits are in season. For the Fourth of July, whole blueberries and sliced strawberries make a gorgeous dessert, but kiwis, raspberries, sliced oranges, mangoes, and peaches are also great choices.

Crust

1 cup real butter (no substitutions!)

1 cup sugar

1 egg (large or extra-large)

1 teaspoon almond extract

3 cups all-purpose flour

1½ teaspoons baking powder

½ teaspoon salt

Zest of 1 orange

Creamy Topping

1 (8-ounce) package cream cheese (light cream cheese is fine)

½ teaspoon orange extract

¼ cup brown sugar

1 cup heavy cream

½ cup powdered sugar

Fruit Topping

4 cups sliced fruit of your choice, washed, cut into small pieces (if necessary), and patted dry

¼ cup dark or semisweet chocolate chips, plus more if desired

1. **For the crust:** Cream butter and sugar until light and fluffy, about 2 minutes. Add egg and extract and mix to incorporate.

2. Lightly spoon flour into measuring cups, level off with a knife, and add to a separate bowl. Add baking powder and salt to the bowl and whisk together.

3. Slowly add flour mixture to butter mixture and stir until completely combined. Mix in orange zest.

4. Spray a round 14-inch or larger pizza pan with nonstick cooking spray and, using your hands and a rolling pin, spread the dough out to the edges of the pan. If desired, you can add a decorative finish (such as fluting) to the edges of the crust. Cover with plastic wrap and refrigerate at least 1 hour.

5. When ready to bake the crust, preheat oven to 350 degrees F. Bake crust 18–25 minutes or until golden brown around the edges and completely baked in the center. For a crisper crust, bake longer. Allow to cool completely.

6. **For the creamy topping:** When crust is almost cool, use an electric mixer to combine cream cheese, orange extract, and brown sugar until light and fluffy. Whip cream and powdered sugar in a separate bowl until medium peaks form. Fold whipped cream into cream cheese mixture and combine well. Spread cream cheese mixture over cooled crust.

7. **For the fruit topping:** Arrange berries and other fruit as desired over the creamy topping. Place chocolate chips in a small, heavy-duty zip-top bag and heat in the microwave 20 seconds at a time, mashing the bag around until chocolate is completely melted and smooth. Cut a small corner off the bag and drizzle chocolate over the berries. Refrigerate pizza until ready to serve and then cut into wedges or squares.

How to Peel and Cut a Kiwi

If you can't seem to get to the sweet and tangy, bright green flesh of a kiwi without mangling it, we're here to help! This method is so safe and easy that you won't ever go back to trying to pare off the furry skin with a knife.

1. Cut off both ends of the kiwi.

2. Take a regular spoon and slip it between the fruit and the skin. Depending on the size of both your fruit and your spoon, you may be able to slide the spoon in all the way to the other side. Otherwise, go halfway, gently working your spoon around the entire kiwi, and then do the same thing from the other end. The skin will easily separate from the fruit, and you can slide it right off. This way you lose hardly any fruit at all.

3. Cut into slices or chunks and serve. Try the Berry-Kiwi Salad with Mint-Lime Dressing (page 21) or put kiwi on Fruit Pizza (page 120).

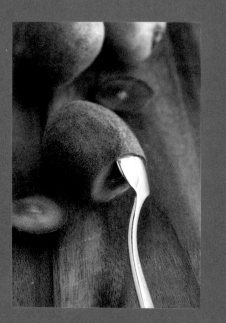

Homemade Fruit Roll-Ups

If you have lots of extra fruit from friends, neighbors, roadside stands, or super-market sales, use it up in these homemade fruit snacks that are so much better for you than what you can get from a box. Plus, kids think it's pretty cool if they get to help make their own lunchbox treats.

2½–3 cups ripe or slightly over-ripe fruit, diced (see Tip 1)

2 teaspoons fresh lemon juice

Spices and/or extracts, to taste, optional

Honey, sugar, or agave, to taste (see Tip 2)

1. Preheat oven to lowest temperature (usually 140–160 degrees F., depending on your oven). Line a baking sheet with microwave-safe plastic wrap or a silicone baking mat (our preference). Don't use foil, parchment, or waxed paper. Set aside.

2. Puree fruit and lemon juice in a food processor or blender until smooth. Add sweetener to taste, along with any desired spices or extracts. Pour onto prepared baking sheet and spread as evenly as possible to about ⅛-inch thick. Place in oven and bake 6–8 hours or until center is not tacky anymore. If edges start to dry out, brush lightly with water to moisten. Remove from oven, let cool to room temperature, and peel off baking sheet. Cut into strips and roll in parchment or plastic wrap. Store in airtight container or freeze.

TIP 1: All fruits will produce slightly different results. Strawberries and raspberries are two of our favorites because they consistently produce great flavor and texture. Experiment with different fruit combinations, spices, and extracts to find what you like best.

TIP 2: The addition of sugar or honey enhances the texture and makes the fruit roll-ups a little more chewy than if you leave it out.

TIP 3: If using plastic wrap: The puree will shrink a little as the fruit dries, so don't spread the fruit puree all the way to the edges, and leave the plastic loose around the edge of your pan.

ROLLOVER
Cream cheese

❋ Author's Note

My kids love making homemade
popsicles and ice cream bars.
You can't really mess up freezing
fresh fruit and flavorful juices, so
I let them pick what they want to
put in, and they love eating their
own creations! This is a great
way to get little ones started in
the kitchen. –Sara

Berry Cheesecake Pops

Take the homemade summer ice pop to a whole new level. These frosty treats combine the sweet flavor of fresh summer berries with the indulgence of creamy cheesecake. Perfect for dessert on a warm summer night or cooling off during a splash fight in the backyard.

2 cups assorted berries, such as strawberries, blueberries, and raspberries

½ cup plus 3 tablespoons powdered sugar, divided

3 ounces cream cheese

1 cup half-and-half

1 teaspoon vanilla

2 teaspoons fresh lemon juice

1. Place berries and 3 tablespoons powdered sugar in a blender or food processor and roughly puree. Taste and add more sugar, if desired. You should have about 1 cup of berry puree, and you can make it as smooth or as chunky as you like.

2. Transfer puree to a bowl or measuring cup with a pour spout and set aside. Wash out blender or food processor and then place cream cheese, half-and-half, vanilla, lemon juice, and ½ cup powdered sugar inside. Puree until smooth.

3. Fill popsicle molds, alternating berry mixture and cream cheese mixture. If desired, stir gently with a popsicle stick for a swirled effect, or leave layered. Freeze until slightly firm. Add a wooden popsicle stick to each mold and then freeze until completely solid.

4. To remove from molds, carefully run the outside of the mold under warm water until popsicles are loosened. Store in an airtight container or zip-top bag in the freezer.

Berry Cobbler

Warm, sweet, citrus-scented dough covers summer's sweetest berries, cooked to syrupy perfection. Top this down-home classic with a high-quality vanilla ice cream or sweetened whipped cream.

Serves 10–12

ROLLOVER
Cream

TIP: You can use frozen berries, just be sure to thaw and drain them before using.

1½ cups all-purpose flour, lightly spooned into the measuring cup and leveled with a knife

⅛ teaspoon salt

1 tablespoon plus ¾ teaspoon baking powder

¾ cup sugar

zest of ½ lemon or orange, optional

¼ cup butter, cold

1 egg

½ cup heavy cream

4 cups fresh berries (we like blueberries and/or blackberries) (see Tip)

¼ cup brown sugar

Streusel Topping

½ cup sugar

¼ cup plus 1 tablespoon flour

1 teaspoon cinnamon

4 tablespoons butter, room temperature

1. Preheat oven to 350 degrees F. Lightly grease a 9 × 13-inch baking dish and set aside.

2. Whisk together flour, salt, baking powder, sugar, and citrus zest in a large mixing bowl. Set aside.

3. Using a cheese shredder, shred butter. Lightly toss the butter with flour mixture until it's mixed evenly and crumbly (don't over-mix here). Whisk the egg and then lightly toss with flour and butter mixture until evenly absorbed. Add in cream and mix until combined; the mixture should be quite sticky and a little lumpy (kind of like biscuit dough). Set aside.

4. Toss berries with brown sugar and spread into the 9 x 13-inch pan. Drop dough over berries and set aside.

5. **For the topping:** Whisk together sugar, flour, and cinnamon. Cut in butter until mixture is crumbly. Sprinkle over dough and bake 45–55 minutes or until the top is golden brown and the crust is cooked through. Serve warm with sweetened whipped cream or vanilla ice cream.

ROLLOVER
Cream

TIP: To toast coconut, sprinkle coconut evenly into a medium-sized skillet and cook over medium heat, stirring frequently, about 8–12 minutes.

Key Lime Trifle

Light, creamy, and unbelievably easy and elegant, this is a perfect addition to backyard get-togethers. Try making it in individual trifle dishes or even tumblers for a fun twist.

1 (4-serving) box vanilla instant pudding mix (can use sugar-free)

½ cup freshly squeezed lime juice

½ cup cold water

1 (14-ounce) can sweetened condensed milk

2 cups heavy cream, divided

1 loaf pound cake or angel food cake, cut into ½-inch cubes

1 cup toasted coconut, divided (see Tip)

⅓ cup powdered sugar

1. Combine pudding mix, lime juice, water, and sweetened condensed milk in a medium-sized bowl. Mix well and refrigerate a few minutes while you prepare the whipped cream.

2. Whip 1 cup cream in another bowl until soft peaks form. Fold into pudding mixture and then return mixture to refrigerator.

3. In a medium trifle dish or small, individual trifle dishes, spread a thin layer of pudding mixture. Add a layer of cake cubes, a thicker layer of pudding, and a sprinkling of coconut. Repeat, ending with a layer of pudding.

4. Whip remaining 1 cup cream with powdered sugar. Spread on top of final layer and garnish with remaining toasted coconut. Chill at least 1 hour before serving.

ROLLOVER
Cream

TIP 1: Room temperature eggs are essential for baking because they tend to mix better and distribute more evenly. To quickly bring eggs to room temperature, place them in a bowl of warm water for a few minutes.

TIP 2: You can also wrap the bottom and sides of the springform pan in a large oven roasting bag before placing in the water pan and immediately before baking. (It sounds weird, but it's a foolproof way to keep water from leaking into the pan.)

Lime-Coconut Cheesecake

Tangy lime and sweet coconut in this creamy cheesecake will instantly transport you somewhere tropical! Be sure to chill this cheesecake for several hours before serving and be prepared to pass out copies of the recipe if you serve it to guests.

Crust

2 cups graham cracker crumbs

½ cup sweetened flaked coconut

2 tablespoons sugar

6 tablespoons butter, melted

Cheesecake

3 (8-ounce) packages cream cheese, softened

1 cup sugar

3 eggs, room temperature (see Tip 1)

1½ teaspoons vanilla extract

2 tablespoons lime zest

½ cup fresh lime juice (about 4–5 medium limes)

Topping

1 cup heavy cream

½ cup powdered sugar

1 teaspoon vanilla extract

1½–2 teaspoons coconut extract

⅓ cup sweetened flaked coconut, toasted (see Tip, page 126)

Lime slices, optional, for garnish

1. Preheat oven to 350 degrees F. Cover the outside bottom and sides of a 9-inch springform pan with a double layer of foil and set aside.

2. **For the crust:** Combine ingredients in a medium-sized bowl and mix well with a fork or your fingers. Press evenly into the bottom of the pan and about 1 inch up the sides. Place pan in oven and bake 5 minutes. Remove and set aside until ready to use.

3. **For the cheesecake:** Beat cream cheese and sugar in a separate bowl until smooth and creamy. Add eggs, one at a time, beating after each addition. Add vanilla, lime zest, and lime juice and beat to combine. Pour batter into prepared crust. Place the wrapped springform pan into a larger pan (such as a roasting pan) and place on center rack of oven. Carefully pour hot water into the larger pan until it reaches about halfway up the springform pan. (See Tip 2.)

4. Bake cheesecake 75–85 minutes or until center is set and the edges just barely begin to brown. Leave cheesecake in oven, but turn heat off and leave oven door open a crack. Allow to sit 30 minutes and then remove and cool completely on a rack. When cooled to room temperature, cover

with plastic wrap and chill overnight. When ready to serve, gently remove edges of the springform pan and place cheesecake on a serving dish.

5. **For the topping:** Beat cream until soft peaks form and then add powdered sugar and extracts. Beat until medium peaks form. Spread whipped cream evenly over cheesecake and sprinkle with toasted coconut. Garnish with sliced limes, if desired. Slice and serve.

Tin Can Treats

Canned fruit with tab tops (we recommend 7- or 8-ounce cans)

Candy, gift cards, or other small treats for filling

Tissue paper

Hot glue gun

Decorative paper (wrapping paper works great)

Ribbon

1. Use a safety or clean-edge can opener to remove bottom of can. If using a traditional can opener, leave can attached at one point.

2. Empty cans (don't forget to eat the fruit!) and wash cans thoroughly. Dry completely.

3. Fill with candies, treats, or trinkets, leaving about ½-inch space at top.

4. Fill remaining space with tissue paper.

5. Use a thin layer of super glue or another glue of your choice to secure the bottom back onto the can. If you used a traditional can opener, hot glue will probably work better.

6. Measure a strip of decorative paper the same height as the can. Wrap around the can and secure with tape or glue.

7. Tie decorative ribbons through the tab on top of can.

8. Attach tag, if desired.

S'mores Cupcakes

This is summer's favorite camping treat in the form of a cupcake! The marshmallow frosting on top of the moist chocolate cupcakes makes this dessert extra amazing.

Makes 14–16 cupcakes

♥ **Family Favorite**

4 graham crackers, plus additional for garnish

1½ teaspoons sugar

2 tablespoons butter

1 recipe Chocolate Cupcakes (page 53)

1 batch Marshmallow Frosting (page 58)

1–2 (5.9-ounce) Hershey's chocolate bars

1. Preheat oven to 350 degrees F. Line a muffin pan with cupcake liners and set aside.

2. Pulse graham crackers in food processor until they become fine crumbs. Add sugar and butter and pulse to combine. Alternately, you could place graham crackers in a heavy-duty zip-top bag and crush with a rolling pin or meat mallet and then mix in sugar and butter. Place about ½ tablespoon graham cracker mixture in the bottom of each cupcake liner and press down lightly with fingertips. Bake 4 minutes and then remove from oven.

3. Fill each cupcake liner with chocolate batter about three-fourths full. Bake 15–20 minutes or until a toothpick comes out with few crumbs attached. Cool in pan 5 minutes and then remove cupcakes from pan and set on wire rack to cool. Cool completely before frosting.

4. Top with marshmallow frosting and sprinkle additional crushed graham crackers on top, if desired. Place 1 section of chocolate bar on top of each cupcake.

Patriotic Cupcakes

Berries, coconut, cake, cream cheese frosting, and patriotic colors—you can't possibly go wrong with this crowd-pleasing dessert!

1 cup shredded coconut, for garnish

1 (18.25-ounce) box white cake mix (disregard instructions on box)

⅓ cup vegetable oil

⅓ cup milk

4 egg whites

1 (6-ounce) carton blueberry yogurt

1 (6-ounce) carton strawberry yogurt

1 (6-ounce) carton coconut yogurt or vanilla yogurt plus ½ teaspoon coconut extract

Red and blue food coloring

Cream cheese frosting of your choice (page 59)

½ teaspoon coconut extract

Fresh strawberries, blueberries, and toasted coconut, for garnish

1. Preheat oven to 350 degrees F.

2. Spread coconut in an even layer on a baking sheet and bake 7–8 minutes, stirring every 2–3 minutes until it's toasted and golden brown. Remove from oven and set aside to cool.

3. Combine cake mix, oil, milk, and egg whites in a mixing bowl and beat 2 minutes, scraping sides of bowl occasionally. Divide the batter evenly into 3 medium-sized mixing bowls. Mix blueberry yogurt and blue food coloring in one bowl of batter until desired color is reached. Mix strawberry yogurt and red food coloring in a second bowl of batter. Mix coconut yogurt, or vanilla yogurt plus coconut extract, into the last bowl of batter and stir to combine.

4. Place cupcake liners in muffin pan. Place 1 tablespoon of 1 color batter in each liner. Use a spoon, or your finger dipped in water, to spread the batter out evenly. Repeat with remaining 2 bowls of batter, layering each color on top of the previous one.

5. Bake about 18–20 minutes or until a toothpick inserted in center comes out clean. Remove from oven and let sit until cool enough to handle. Remove cupcakes from pan and cool completely to room temperature.

6. Prepare cream cheese frosting of your choice, adding in the coconut flavor.

7. Frost the cupcakes and top with fresh berries and toasted coconut.

Glazed Maple Pecan Cookies, see page 193

Autumn

WHAT WE LOVE

- bonfires
- football games
- roasting marshmallows
- kicking and crunching through dry leaves
- warm, sunny days and clear, chilly nights
- crisp apples
- the smell of cinnamon from the kitchen and of burning leaves from the yard
- warming up with hot spiced cider after a night of trick-or-treating
- the scent of hay and horses on a hayride through the pumpkin patch

HALLOWEEN

Thanksgiving

IN SEASON

Apples, butternut squash, cauliflower, cranberries, ginger, pears, pumpkin

AUTUMN

Homemade Dulce de Leche

Try serving this super-easy Latin treat as a fruit dip; as a spread on bread, crackers, or cookies; as a topping for your favorite ice cream; as a cupcake filling; swirled into frosting or hot chocolate; or licked straight off the spoon. We love it on crisp apple slices.

1 (14-ounce) can sweetened condensed milk

1. Preheat oven to 425 degrees F. Pour sweetened condensed milk into a shallow baking dish, such as a pie plate. Cover very tightly with foil, making sure all sides are covered and sealed.

2. Place baking dish in a larger pan, such as a roasting pan. Fill larger pan with hot water until water level reaches about halfway up the baking dish. Bake about 60 minutes and then check. Color should be a rich caramel brown. Continue baking if necessary, checking every 15 minutes. It may take up to 90 minutes or more to reach proper level of doneness. When a medium caramel color is reached, remove from oven and let cool. Whisk until smooth. Store in refrigerator.

♥ **Family Favorite**

🌸 *Author's Note*

I love packaging dulce de leche in cute jars for gifts. I also like gifting them to people who have a high probability of sharing them with me. —*Sara*

Apple-Cinnamon Cream Cheese Bites

These tasty little bites combine some of our favorite things—freshly baked bread, cream cheese, and apples with cinnamon. If you have a little extra time on your hands, use your favorite roll or cinnamon roll recipe in place of the refrigerated French bread dough.

4 ounces cream cheese

6 tablespoons powdered sugar

1 teaspoon almond extract

1 medium to large tart green apple, peeled and diced (about 1¼–1½ cups)

1 tablespoon flour

1½ tablespoons sugar

1½ tablespoons brown sugar

1 teaspoon lemon juice

½ teaspoon cinnamon

1 roll ready-to-bake refrigerated French bread dough

Glaze

1 tablespoon melted butter

¼ cup powdered sugar

¼ teaspoon almond extract

1–2 tablespoons milk (to reach desired consistency)

1. Preheat oven to 375 degrees F.

2. Beat together cream cheese, powdered sugar, and almond extract in a medium-sized bowl until light and fluffy.

3. Toss apple pieces with flour, sugar, brown sugar, lemon juice, and cinnamon in another bowl until they're well coated.

4. On a lightly floured surface, roll bread dough into a 9 x 12-inch rectangle. Using a pizza cutter or sharp knife, cut the longer side into 4 equal rows. Cut the shorter side into 3 equal rows, creating twelve 3 x 3-inch squares.

5. Lightly spray a 12-cup muffin pan with nonstick spray. Place 1 square of bread dough in each of the cups.

6. Evenly distribute cream cheese mixture into the dough-lined muffin cups and spread out evenly. Top with apple mixture.

7. Bake 15–20 minutes or until bread is light golden brown. Remove from oven and let pan cool 5–10 minutes. Use a fork to carefully remove apple bites from the pan and place on a cooling rack.

8. **For glaze:** Whisk together glaze ingredients and drizzle over each apple bite.

ROLLOVER
Buttermilk

TIP: For best results use hard white wheat flour (it's still whole wheat flour, just a different variety than most people are used to), bread flour, and vital wheat gluten because they all help ensure the rolls don't become heavy or hard. Vital wheat gluten can be found in specialty kitchen or baking shops or the baking aisle or health food section of well-stocked grocery stores.

Hearty Whole-Grain Crescent Rolls

These seeded whole-grain rolls are a little extra work, but the end result is a light, fluffy, nutty roll that will make believers out of even the most ardent white bread fans.

¾ cup warm (105–115 degrees F.) water

1 tablespoon sugar

1 tablespoon bread machine yeast

3 tablespoons flax seed, divided (or 2 tablespoons ground flax seed and 1 tablespoon whole flax seed)

3 tablespoons unsalted, shelled sunflower seeds, divided

3 tablespoons sesame seeds, divided

2½ tablespoons poppy seeds, divided

1½ cups buttermilk

2 tablespoons melted butter

3 tablespoons honey

2 teaspoons salt

3 cups hard white wheat flour (see Tip)

2 tablespoons vital wheat gluten

2–3 cups bread flour

1 egg white

2 tablespoons cold water

2 tablespoons uncooked oats

1. Combine warm water and sugar in a small bowl. Sprinkle on yeast, stir to combine, and allow to stand 10 minutes or until frothy.

2. While yeast is proofing, combine 2 tablespoons each of flax, sunflower, and sesame seeds and ½ tablespoon of poppy seeds in a small skillet, reserving the remainder to top the rolls. Toast over medium heat, stirring frequently, until fragrant and the sesame seeds start to turn a light golden color.

3. Combine buttermilk, melted butter, honey, and salt in the bowl of a heavy-duty mixer. Add yeast mixture and mix well. Combine hard white wheat flour, vital wheat gluten, and toasted seeds in a separate bowl and then add to yeast mixture and mix well. Add bread flour, ½ cup at a time, until dough pulls away from the sides of the bowl and it barely sticks to your finger. At that point, mix in mixer for 5 minutes.

4. Spray a large glass or metal bowl with nonstick cooking spray. When dough is kneaded, turn dough into bowl and cover with a clean dish cloth. Allow to rise in a warm place until doubled, about 1 hour.

5. Lightly flour a work surface (or spray with nonstick cooking spray). Line 2 baking sheets with Silpat liners or parchment paper and set aside.

6. When dough has risen, transfer to work surface and divide in half. Roll each half into a circle about 12 inches in diameter and about ¼–½-inch thick. Using a pizza wheel or a dough cutter, cut the dough into 8 equal wedges. Starting with the wide edge of each wedge, roll down to the point. Place on baking sheet and form into a slight crescent. Repeat with remaining dough pieces. Cover and allow to rise until doubled, about 45 minutes. When the dough has about 10 minutes left to rise, preheat oven to 375 degrees F.

7. Whisk together the egg white and water. Mix reserved seeds and oats in a small bowl. When the rolls are done rising, carefully brush tops of each with egg white mixture. Sprinkle evenly with seeds and bake 13–15 minutes or until barely golden brown on top. Bake them one sheet at a time (which we recommend) or rotate the sheets halfway through the baking time. If possible, serve warm with butter.

♥ **Family Favorite**

☺ **Quick and Easy**

ROLLOVER
Sour cream

VARIATION: Omit Streusel Topping and pipe your favorite cream cheese frosting on top of muffins.

Streusel-Topped Pumpkin Chocolate Chip Muffins

No one will ever guess how easy these spectacular muffins are to make! Using a high-quality cake mix ensures fantastic results every time, regardless of elevation or baking experience.

1 (18.25-ounce) spice cake mix (we prefer Duncan Hines)

1 (15-ounce) can pumpkin

1 cup sour cream

¼ cup vegetable oil

3 eggs

1 teaspoon vanilla

1 (12-ounce) package chocolate chips

Streusel Topping

¼ cup all-purpose flour

½ cup sugar

1 teaspoon pumpkin pie spice

3 tablespoons butter

1. Ignore directions on the cake mix box. Preheat oven to 350 degrees F. Line two 12-cup muffin tins with cupcake liners and set aside.

2. Combine cake mix, pumpkin, sour cream, oil, eggs, and vanilla in a large bowl or the bowl of a stand mixer. Mix 30 seconds on low or until all ingredients have been moistened and then beat 2–3 minutes on medium speed or until the batter is smooth. Mix in chocolate chips. Divide batter evenly into cupcake liners.

3. **For the topping:** Whisk together flour, sugar, and pumpkin pie spice and then cut in butter with 2 knives until mixture resembles coarse crumbs. Sprinkle topping over batter.

4. Bake muffins 20–30 minutes or until tops are golden brown and a toothpick inserted into the center of a muffin comes out completely clean. Cool on a wire rack before serving.

Chunky Monkey Pancakes

These light and fluffy pancakes have become a blog sensation! Dotted with chunks of sweet banana and decadent chocolate and drizzled with a unique peanut butter syrup, they will have all of the monkeys in your life begging for more!

Makes 28–30 small pancakes or 14–15 medium pancakes

♥ **Family Favorite**

ROLLOVER
Buttermilk

FREEZER INSTRUCTIONS:
Let cooked pancakes cool to room temperature. Place in a single layer in the freezer until frozen and then place pancakes in a zip-top bag or airtight container. Reheat in a microwave or toaster until heated through.

TIP: If you don't have any buttermilk, place 1½ tablespoons lemon juice or white vinegar in a liquid measuring cup and then fill to 1½ cups with milk and let stand 5 minutes.

1½ cups flour

3 tablespoons sugar

2 teaspoons baking powder

1½ teaspoons baking soda

¼ teaspoon salt

1½ cups buttermilk (see Tip)

1 large or extra large egg

1 tablespoon canola oil

1 teaspoon vanilla extract

2 small to medium ripe bananas

6 tablespoons mini chocolate chips (or regular chocolate chips, roughly chopped) tossed with 2 teaspoons flour

Cooking spray or butter for pan

1. Combine flour, sugar, baking powder, baking soda, and salt in a mixing bowl and whisk together. Mix buttermilk, egg, oil, and vanilla in a separate bowl and whisk well. Add wet ingredients to the dry ingredients and mix just until moistened and combined. Place bananas in a bowl and roughly mash with a fork. Fold into batter. Add chocolate chips that have been tossed with flour and then stir.

2. Heat a nonstick griddle or skillet to medium heat. Coat pan with a little butter or cooking spray and then pour on pancake batter. Use ¼ cup batter for large pancakes (4–6 inch) and 2 tablespoons for kid-sized ones (2–3 inch). Wait until bubbles form and edges are set and then flip. Reheat syrup, if necessary, and pour over warm pancakes.

Maple-Peanut Butter Syrup

½ cup creamy peanut butter

1 cup 100% real maple syrup

Heat peanut butter 30 seconds in the microwave. Add maple syrup and gently whisk to combine. Heat in the microwave another 30 seconds, whisk, and then set aside.

Author's Note

When I was young, a friend introduced me to peanut butter and maple syrup on pancakes, and it's been a favorite combination ever since. I literally dreamed of this creation one night, and when I woke up in the morning, I sprinted to my kitchen to see if they tasted as amazing in real life as they did in my sleep. Sure enough! If only they were calorie-free, like they were in my dream. —Sara

☆ **Make Ahead**

ROLLOVERS
Celery
Green onions

Author's Note

One of my parents' favorite lunch spots always served chicken salad with grapes. I assumed that was how everyone ate their chicken salad. I love the bites of juicy sweetness, especially with crunchy celery and tangy dressing. — Kate

Orchard Chicken Salad

Sweet, juicy grapes and crisp apples combine with tender chicken and a tangy dressing for an easy chicken salad that you can make up to a few days ahead of time.

1 pound grilled chicken breasts, chopped into bite-sized pieces

¼ cup chopped green onions

1 cup (about 2 large stalks) chopped celery

1 cup chopped sweet crisp apple, such as Gala or Honeycrisp

¾ cup mayonnaise

1 tablespoon Creole or other mild coarse-grained mustard

Kosher salt and freshly ground black pepper, to taste

1 cup halved grapes

½ cup chopped pecans, toasted

Combine chicken, onions, celery, and apple in a large bowl. Whisk together mayonnaise and mustard in a small bowl and then add it to chicken mixture and toss to combine. Season with salt and pepper, to taste. Chill for several hours (up to 2 days). Right before serving, add grapes and pecans. Serve on croissants, in pitas, or wrapped in tortillas with a leaf of crisp lettuce.

Holiday Quinoa Salad

If you've never had quinoa before, it's a source of hearty, protein-packed complex carbohydrates that's similar in texture to rice. In fact, we often substitute it for rice and, so far, our kids haven't complained! This salad is a great healthy choice to offer guests during the holiday season.

Serves 6–8

☺ **Quick and Easy**
🌿 **Vegetarian**

ROLLOVERS
Feta cheese
Green onions

2 cups water or chicken broth

1 cup uncooked quinoa

½ cup crumbled feta cheese

½ cup chopped pecans, toasted

½ cup chopped green onions

½ cup dried cranberries

Zest of 1 orange

Citrus Dressing

1. Bring water or chicken broth to a boil in a medium saucepan. Add quinoa and cover with a tight-fitting lid. Reduce heat to simmer and cook 20 minutes. Remove from heat, allow to stand 5 minutes and then fluff with a fork. Chill.

2. Toss chilled quinoa, feta cheese, pecans, green onions, cranberries, and orange zest together. Drizzle Citrus Dressing over the mixture and then toss quickly to combine. Serve cold.

Citrus Dressing

¼ cup freshly squeezed orange juice

2 tablespoons olive or canola oil

1 clove garlic, minced

½ teaspoon kosher salt

10 cracks black pepper

2 teaspoons Creole or other mild coarse-grained mustard

Whisk ingredients together. If possible, refrigerate at least 1 hour before serving.

Chicken and Wild Rice Soup

Serves 10–12

ROLLOVERS
Celery
Mushrooms

Our lightened-up take on this classic recipe has become a favorite with our families and the families we share it with! Use leftover rotisserie chicken for quick and easy preparation.

5 tablespoons butter, divided

1 onion, chopped

4 cloves garlic, minced or pressed

1 cup chopped carrots (about 2 medium)

2 cups roughly chopped portabella or baby bella mushrooms

2 stalks celery, chopped

½ teaspoon poultry seasoning

1 (12-ounce) jar marinated artichoke hearts, drained and chopped

8 cups chicken broth or 8 cups water plus 2 tablespoons and 2 teaspoons chicken base

1 cup wild rice

2 (6-ounce) boneless, skinless chicken breasts, cooked and cubed (can also use leftover rotisserie chicken)

½ teaspoon kosher salt

¼ teaspoon freshly ground black pepper

½ cup flour

2 cups milk

1. Melt 1 tablespoon butter in a large stockpot over medium heat. Add onion, garlic, carrots, mushrooms, celery, and poultry seasoning and sauté until onion is translucent, about 5 minutes. Add artichoke hearts and chicken broth and bring to a boil over high heat. Add rice and chicken, reduce heat, cover, and simmer 50–60 minutes or until rice is tender. When rice is tender, remove from heat and add salt and pepper.

2. When the soup has about 10 minutes left, melt remaining 4 tablespoons butter in a small saucepan over medium-low heat. Whisk in flour to make a roux. Slowly add milk, about ½ cup at a time, whisking constantly to remove lumps, until smooth and thickened to the consistency of thin pudding. Slowly whisk milk mixture into the soup and stir until combined. Simmer 4–5 minutes, until slightly thickened.

Weeknight Chili

Everyone needs a recipe for a slow-simmering chili for snowy afternoons, but everyone also needs a recipe for a quick, easy, healthy meal and this is the one! Even our pickiest eaters love this chili, especially when we let them add shredded cheese.

1 pound lean ground beef

1 medium onion, chopped

1 green pepper, chopped

3–4 cloves garlic, minced

1 (15-ounce) can light kidney, black, or pinto beans, drained

1 (14.5-ounce) can diced tomatoes, undrained

1 (8-ounce) can tomato sauce

1 (15-ounce) can beef broth

1 tablespoon chili powder

½ teaspoon Italian seasoning

Salt and pepper, to taste

Tabasco sauce or cayenne pepper, to taste, optional

Shredded cheddar cheese and/or chopped white or yellow onions, for garnish

Serves 6–8

⊙ **Quick and Easy**

❋ *Author's Note*

This is the dinner standard for my picky eater—if we're having something new, he'll ask if it's even close to as good as this chili. Of course, I tell him it always is since I'm trying to get him to try new foods. — *Kate*

1. In a large stockpot, brown the ground beef. When the beef is about halfway cooked, drain fat, if necessary, and then add onion, pepper, and garlic and cook until onion is translucent. Add beans, tomatoes, tomato sauce, broth, chili powder, and Italian seasoning and bring to a boil. Cover and reduce heat; simmer 20–30 minutes (or longer, if you have time). Season to taste with salt and pepper. If you want a little heat, add some Tabasco sauce or cayenne pepper.

2. Garnish with shredded cheddar cheese or chopped onion, and serve with your favorite cracker.

Tortellini Sausage Soup

This recipe from our friend Jen has become a family favorite for both of us, as well as a favorite of our blog readers. It's loaded with vegetables, it's hearty and satisfying, and we've never met anyone who didn't like it. This, along with a loaf of garlic bread or a batch of breadsticks, is Kate's go-to meal when taking dinners to friends and neighbors.

3 links Italian sausage

1 onion, diced

4 cloves garlic, pressed or minced

1 (14.5-ounce) can diced tomatoes

1 (8-ounce) can tomato sauce

½ cup apple cider (don't leave this out!)

½ cup water

2 (15-ounce) cans chicken broth

1 cup sliced carrots

1 teaspoon dried oregano

1 teaspoon dried basil

2 tablespoons dried parsley

2 medium zucchini, shredded (a great way to use your food processor if you have one)

1 (8–10-ounce) package cheese tortellini (see Tip)

Parmesan cheese

1. Remove the casings from link sausage. Use a sharp knife to cut a slit down one side of the sausage and then peel back the casing. Crumble sausage into a large soup pot and begin cooking it over medium heat.

2. Add onion and garlic to the pot. Continue cooking until onion is translucent, the sausage is cooked, and your house smells like heaven.

3. Add tomatoes, tomato sauce, apple cider, water, chicken broth, carrots, oregano, and basil. Cover and simmer ½ hour. Add parsley and zucchini and simmer another 15 minutes or so. Add tortellini and cook until tender. Serve with bread and freshly grated Parmesan cheese.

Orange-Cranberry Pork Tenderloin

The sweetness of the orange and the tartness of the cranberry are perfect complements for lean, tender pork in this healthy dinner that will get you in the mood for falling leaves and cooler weather!

2 pork tenderloins (1–1½ pounds total—pork tenderloins are usually packaged in pairs)

1 teaspoon garlic powder

1 teaspoon onion powder

2 teaspoons kosher salt

½ teaspoon freshly cracked black pepper

1½ tablespoons extra virgin olive oil

1 (14-ounce) can whole berry cranberry sauce

Juice of 1 orange (about ¼ cup)

Zest of 1 orange

3 cloves garlic, minced or pressed

1 tablespoon Creole or other mild coarse-grained mustard

½ cup chicken broth

1. Preheat oven to 400 degrees F.

2. Rinse pork in cold water and pat dry with paper towels. Mix together garlic powder, onion powder, salt, and pepper in a small bowl and then sprinkle evenly over all sides of pork.

3. Heat a large, oven-safe skillet to medium-high heat. Add oil and tilt pan until oil coats the bottom. Use tongs to place tenderloins in pan and sear 1–2 minutes on each side or until golden brown.

4. While pork is searing, whisk together cranberry sauce, orange juice, orange zest, garlic, mustard, and chicken broth. When pork is seared on all sides (it's okay if some pink remains), pour sauce into pan and bring to a simmer, scraping bottom of pan while sauce simmers 1 minute.

5. Place skillet in oven, uncovered, and cook 20–30 minutes or until internal temperature of pork tenderloins reaches 150 degrees F. Remove from oven and let rest 5 minutes. Place pork on cutting board and slice into ½-inch slices. Return to pan and serve with extra sauce drizzled over the top.

Author's Note

Sara and I are notoriously clumsy in the kitchen. This recipe wouldn't be the same if we didn't burn ourselves on the hot pan handle every single time we pull it out of the oven. Learn from our mistakes! Do what apparently we cannot do! Slip a hot pad over the handle after you pull it out of the oven so you don't forget the handle is hot! — Kate

Apple Butter Pork Chops

A little sweet and tangy, these spiced pork chops smothered in caramelized onions are a perfect dinner for a cool autumn evening. Serve with rice and steamed vegetables or a tossed green salad.

¼ cup all-purpose flour

½ teaspoon kosher salt

½ teaspoon black pepper

½ teaspoon garlic powder

1 tablespoon olive oil

4 lean, boneless pork chops (see Tip)

1 cup high-quality apple cider

¼ cup apple butter

1 tablespoon water

1 teaspoon pressed garlic

1½ tablespoons Creole or mild coarse-grained mustard

1 recipe Caramelized Onions (page 117)

1. Preheat oven to 375 degrees F.

2. Combine flour, salt, pepper, and garlic powder together in a small bowl. Heat oil in a large, oven-safe skillet over medium-high heat. Dredge pork chops in flour mixture and then brown them 2–3 minutes on each side until they're brown and crispy.

3. While pork chops are browning, combine apple cider, apple butter, water, garlic, and mustard. When pork chops are ready, add cider mixture to the pan and cook 1–2 minutes or until sauce begins to evaporate and thicken. Remove from heat and distribute caramelized onions evenly over the pork chops. Cover the pan with a lid and bake 30 minutes.

Author's Note

I've slightly adapted this recipe that has been in my family for years. It would often make an appearance on special occasions, such as holidays and birthdays, or when we had company over. I still have memories from my childhood of the smell of savory roast filling our home and my mother stirring up the sweet and tangy sauce. —*Sara*

Oven-Roasted Barbecue Brisket

This slow-roasted brisket in a sweet and savory sauce is tender enough to pull apart with a fork, and leftovers are even better. This recipe isn't hard or work-intensive, but it cooks over a period of two days, so plan ahead! Serve it on rolls as sandwiches or over rice or mashed potatoes with sauce spooned on top. Pair either one with a tossed green salad for a hearty meal. This recipe can easily be doubled for a large, 8–10-pound brisket.

4–5 pounds beef brisket (not the pickled, corned beef kind; ask the butcher if you have any questions)

Kosher salt

Freshly cracked black pepper

Sauce

4 tablespoons butter

1 large onion, diced

4 cloves garlic, minced

¾ cup water

2 cups ketchup

3 tablespoons fresh lemon juice

6 tablespoons brown sugar

2 tablespoons apple cider vinegar

2 tablespoons Dijon mustard

2 teaspoons kosher salt

1 tablespoon liquid smoke

6 tablespoons Worcestershire sauce

Dash cayenne pepper

1. **First day:** Preheat oven to 275 degrees F.

2. Rinse the brisket in cool water and pat dry with paper towels. Salt and pepper both sides generously and place fat side up in a large roasting pan. Place lid on pan or cover tightly with foil. Cook about 5 hours.

3. Remove from oven and let rest until roast is cool enough to handle. Remove roast from the pan and place on a cutting board. Scrape bits from bottom of pan and strain all pan drippings into a fat separator or glass bowl or jar. Let sit for a few minutes to allow fat to separate and then skim off fat and discard. Scrape fat layer off the roast and discard. Place roast back into empty roasting pan. Let cool to room temperature, cover pan with foil, and refrigerate overnight. Place reserved meat juices in refrigerator in a separate container.

4. **Second day:** Prepare sauce. Heat a large stockpot to medium heat. Add butter, and when melted, add onion and garlic. Sauté, stirring occasionally

until soft and tender, about 4–5 minutes. Add water, ketchup, lemon juice, brown sugar, vinegar, mustard, salt, liquid smoke, Worcestershire sauce, and cayenne pepper. Add up to 2 cups reserved meat juices. Bring sauce to a boil and reduce to simmer. Simmer 20 minutes. While sauce is simmering, slice roast in ½-inch slices. Carefully set meat back in roasting pan and pour sauce over it. Cook 1 hour, basting occasionally.

Sunday Beef Stew

Serves 8–10

🍲 **Slow Cooker**

ROLLOVER
Celery

TIP: A pair of kitchen shears will make trimming the stew meat into smaller pieces quick and easy.

❋ *Author's Note*

For years, we would put this stew in the oven before we went to church, and it would be ready when we got home. I never tired of this particular tradition.

—*Kate*

In this recipe, bite-sized pieces of beef simmer slowly in a tomato-based broth with carrots, onions, garlic, and potatoes. The result is rich and comforting, perfect for a chilly fall or winter evening. Serve with breadsticks, warm rolls, thick slices of whole wheat bread, or in bread bowls.

1½–2 pounds lean stew beef, cut into even smaller bite-sized pieces

4–5 medium red potatoes, chopped

4–5 medium carrots, peeled and chopped

4 stalks celery, chopped

2 onions, chopped

4–5 cloves garlic, minced

2 (12-ounce) cans or 3 cups vegetable juice cocktail, such as V8

1 (10-ounce) can condensed tomato soup

10 ounces water (use the tomato soup can to measure)

1 teaspoon dried basil

2 beef bouillon cubes (or 2 teaspoons beef base)

½ teaspoon freshly ground black pepper

1. Preheat oven to 350 degrees F.

2. Combine all ingredients in a Dutch oven or a heavy, oven-safe pot with a lid. Cover, place in preheated oven, and cook 3 hours.

3. Remove from oven and serve.

Swedish Meatballs

If you've ever been to Ikea, you've probably had their famous Swedish meatballs. Kate's husband spent two years in Scandinavia as a missionary, so these meatballs had to get his final approval before they could make it into the cookbook!

½ cup panko bread crumbs

1 cup buttermilk

1 pound ground beef (85% lean)

1 pound ground pork

1 egg, lightly beaten

¾ cup minced onion, pressed between paper towels to remove excess moisture

¼ cup capers, chopped

2 tablespoons Creole mustard

1½ teaspoons kosher salt

½ teaspoon black pepper

3 cloves garlic, minced

2 tablespoons finely minced fresh parsley

3 tablespoons butter

⅓ cup all-purpose flour

3 cups low-sodium beef broth

3–4 tablespoons cream, optional

Salt and pepper, to taste

Makes about 50 small meatballs; serves 6–8

♥ **Family Favorite**

ROLLOVERS
Buttermilk
Cream
Parsley

TIP: This gravy doesn't actually need cream to be thick and creamy, but it's a delicious addition if you have some in the refrigerator.

1. Line a rimmed baking sheet with aluminum foil. Set aside.

2. Combine bread crumbs and buttermilk in a large bowl and allow to stand 10 minutes. Add beef, pork, egg, onion, capers, mustard, salt, pepper, garlic, and parsley and combine with your hands. Using a cookie scoop, scoop meat mixture into tablespoon-sized portions and shape into balls. Place on baking sheet. Broil 10–12 minutes on low or until meatballs are brown on top.

3. While meatballs are browning, melt butter in a large saucepan over medium-low heat. Add flour and whisk until smooth. Add about 1 cup beef broth and whisk together until completely smooth. Add remaining beef broth and increase heat to medium so the gravy begins to simmer and thicken. Add browned meatballs and simmer about 15 minutes. Remove from heat, and if desired, stir in cream. Season with additional salt and pepper, if needed. Serve with chopped fresh parsley; boiled red potatoes tossed with butter, salt, and pepper; and lingonberry or whole cranberry sauce.

Tuna Noodle Casserole

This updated recipe brings new life to an old family classic, and it's sure to be a favorite of both children and adults.

4 tablespoons butter, divided

1 medium stalk celery, thinly sliced or diced

¼ cup diced onion

8 ounces mushrooms, sliced or diced

Olive oil, as needed

4 tablespoons flour

1 (14.5-ounce) can chicken broth (just under 2 cups), warmed

1 cup milk, warmed

¼ teaspoon salt

¼ teaspoon black pepper

⅛ teaspoon dried dill weed

2 teaspoons fresh lemon juice, plus more if desired

2 tablespoons fresh minced parsley

1 cup freshly grated Parmesan cheese, divided

1 (8-ounce) package medium shell pasta, cooked al dente according to package directions

1 (5-ounce) can tuna, packed in water (double if desired)

¼ cup Ritz cracker crumbs mixed with about ½ tablespoon melted butter or ¼–½ cup crushed potato chips

1. Preheat oven to 350 degrees F. Melt 1 tablespoon butter in a large skillet. Add celery and sauté 2–3 minutes. Add onion and cook 2–3 minutes longer, stirring often. Add mushrooms and cook 3–5 minutes more until mushrooms are golden and tender. If needed for moisture, drizzle a little olive oil over the mushrooms, adding more oil if needed during remaining cooking time. Remove vegetables from pan and set aside.

2. Melt remaining 3 tablespoons butter in pan and add flour. Stir constantly for 30 seconds. Add broth and milk a little at a time while constantly whisking until mixture is smooth. Bring to a low simmer. Add salt, pepper, and dill. Stir constantly until thickened and bubbly, about 2–3 minutes. Reduce heat to low and add lemon juice, parsley, and ½ cup Parmesan cheese. Whisk until smooth. Season with additional salt, pepper, and lemon juice, to taste. Remove from heat and add pasta, vegetables, and tuna. Stir to combine and transfer to a 3-quart baking dish sprayed lightly with cooking spray. Sprinkle with remaining cheese (add more if you want) and sprinkle cracker crumbs or chips on top.

3. Bake 25–30 minutes, until top is golden and pasta is hot and bubbly. Let rest 10–15 minutes before serving to allow sauce to thicken.

Thanksgiving Turkey

We've brined, we've bagged, and we've injected turkeys with flavoring, so we figured if one of those was good, all three would be better! And we were right. This will soon become a family-favorite Thanksgiving staple, and people will talk about your moist, flavorful turkey for months to come. We promise.

Serves 10–12

ROLLOVERS
Celery
Parsley
Rosemary
Sage

SUPPLIES:
- 1 (5-gallon) bucket and lid (washed well)
- A reliable oven-safe meat thermometer
- Flavor injector/meat syringe
- Turkey-size oven roasting bags
- Heavy-duty roasting pan

TIP: Give yourself a week or more between buying and roasting your turkey to make sure your turkey roasting experience goes off without a hitch.

---

1 turkey, no larger than 12–14 pounds

16 cups plus ½ cup chicken broth, divided

1 tablespoon whole peppercorns

½ cup brown or white sugar

1 cup kosher salt

5–6 cloves garlic, mashed

1 tablespoon dried minced onion

1 large sprig fresh thyme

1 large sprig fresh sage

1 large sprig fresh rosemary

1 handful fresh parsley

8 cups cold water

8 cups ice

¾ cup butter, divided

1 tablespoon chopped fresh sage

2–3 cloves garlic

1 apple, cut in half

1–2 small onions, cut in half

4 stalks celery, cut into thirds

1. About a week before you begin brining the turkey, place it in the refrigerator to defrost.

2. The day before you roast the turkey, combine 16 cups chicken broth and next 9 ingredients in a large stockpot. Bring to a boil and then remove from heat and allow to cool to room temperature.

3. Remove packaging from turkey. Remove neck and giblets (be sure to check both body and neck cavities) and reserve for later use, if desired. Rinse turkey in cool water and then place in a 5-gallon bucket. Add cold water and ice cubes and then add brine mixture. Stir to combine. Cover bucket with a lid and set in a cold place up to 24 hours.

4. When you're ready to roast the turkey, preheat oven according to directions on oven bag packaging. Soften ½ cup butter, mix in sage, and set aside. Remove turkey from the brine, rinse in cool water, and place in roasting pan. Gently loosen skin covering turkey breast and slide your hand underneath it to separate breast from skin. (Use a rubber glove for this step if you're squeamish!) Spread handfuls of sage butter between breast and skin, rubbing any excess over the outside of skin.

5. Combine ½ cup chicken broth, 2–3 cloves garlic, and ¼ cup melted butter in a blender until completely smooth. Use flavor injector to inject mixture all over turkey.

6. Slip any remaining rosemary and thyme sprigs under skin.

7. Stuff apple, onion, and celery into turkey cavity. Insert meat thermometer into thickest part of turkey breast and then place turkey in oven roasting bag and roast according to package directions until thermometer registers 165 degrees F. Remove turkey from oven and cut bag away. Allow to stand 15–20 minutes before slicing to allow juices to redistribute. Carve and enjoy (but be sure to snap a picture first)!

Cranberry Sauce

Cranberry sauce seems to be a love-it-or-hate-it dish that's required on every Thanksgiving table. We love it with Thanksgiving Turkey (page 160), Swedish Meatballs (page 157), pulled turkey or pork, or on top of ice cream or cobbler. It's also an amazing spread on homemade bread for day-after-Thanksgiving turkey sandwiches. Freeze any extras in small quantities and then thaw them as you need them.

1 (12-ounce) bag cranberries

1 cup water

1 pinch ground cloves, optional

1 stick cinnamon, optional

1 cup orange juice

1 cup sugar

1. Preheat oven to 350 degrees F.

2. Wash cranberries and place in a 9 x 13-inch baking dish. Add water, cloves, cinnamon stick, and orange juice, and sprinkle with sugar. Bake 1 hour.

3. Remove from oven, remove cinnamon stick, and allow to cool. If you like it with a little texture, mash berries; if you prefer it smooth, process in blender or food processor until desired consistency is reached.

Grilled Turkey and Cranberry Sandwich

4 tablespoons mayonnaise

1 teaspoon red wine vinegar

1–2 tablespoons fresh minced sage leaves

2 cracks black pepper

2 slices rustic white sandwich bread

Roast turkey slices

2–3 tablespoons Cranberry Sauce

4 slices creamy white cheese, such as Brie or baby Swiss

Combine mayonnaise, vinegar, sage, and pepper. Spread desired amount on bread slices. Layer turkey slices and top with Cranberry Sauce and cheese. Grill on a panini press or in a hot buttered skillet, flipping once, until golden brown on both sides.

Herbed Sourdough Stuffing

This stuffing uses sourdough bread, fresh lemons, and herbs and will be a welcome change in tradition to any Thanksgiving table!

Serves 8–10

ROLLOVERS
Celery
Parsley
Rosemary
Sage

1 pound sliced rustic sourdough bread, cut into 1-inch squares

8 tablespoons butter (no substitutions)

1 cup diced celery

1 small to medium onion, diced

5 cloves garlic, pressed or finely minced

1 teaspoon kosher salt

¼ teaspoon black pepper

6 tablespoons minced fresh sage

1 tablespoon minced fresh rosemary, or 1 teaspoon dried crushed rosemary

¼ teaspoon ground marjoram

2 medium lemons (you'll need ¼ cup lemon juice and 2 teaspoons grated lemon zest)

¼ cup fresh minced parsley

1 cup chicken broth, plus more if needed

1. Preheat oven to 400 degrees F. Place bread cubes on a large rimmed baking sheet (2 if needed) and toast bread 10–12 minutes until lightly toasted. When finished, remove pan and reduce oven temperature to 350 degrees F.

2. Melt butter in a large skillet on medium heat. Add celery, onion, garlic, salt, and pepper. Sauté 6–7 minutes, stirring frequently, and then add sage, rosemary, and marjoram. Cook another 2–3 minutes or until celery and onion are tender.

3. Remove from heat and stir in lemon zest, lemon juice, and parsley. Place toasted bread cubes in a large bowl. Add vegetable mixture and toss together, slowly adding chicken broth while tossing. Add additional broth as needed for desired moisture content.

4. Place mixture in a baking dish (9 x 9-inch or 9 x 13-inch works well) and bake 20 minutes. Gently toss mixture and then bake an additional 20 minutes until lightly browned on top. Cover with foil if getting too brown.

Homemade Green Bean Casserole

This is a fresh, condensed-soup-free version of the classic Thanksgiving side dish. Home-fried Crispy Shoestring Onions are the delicious, indulgent proverbial icing on the cake.

2 pounds fresh green beans, trimmed and cut into 2–3-inch pieces

4 tablespoons butter, divided

3 cloves garlic, pressed or minced

3 tablespoons grated onion

1 cup sliced cremini mushrooms

3 tablespoons flour

1 cup beef broth

½ teaspoon kosher salt

¼ teaspoon black pepper

½ teaspoon Worcestershire sauce

½ cup half-and-half

1½ cups Crispy Shoestring Onions, more if desired (page 108)

1. Bring a large pot of water to a boil and add green beans. Cook until crisp-tender, about 5 minutes. Remove from boiling water and immediately plunge beans into ice water. Drain and lay on paper towels to absorb excess water.

2. Heat 2 tablespoons butter in a large skillet over medium heat. Add garlic, onion, and mushrooms and cook, stirring frequently, until mushrooms are tender and golden, about 3–4 minutes. Use a spatula to move mushrooms over to one side of pan. Add remaining 2 tablespoons butter to empty side of pan. When melted, add flour, and stir with spatula for 1 minute. Slowly add beef broth, whisking to eliminate lumps, until mixture is smooth. Add salt, pepper, and Worcestershire sauce. Stir mushroom mixture into sauce and bring to a simmer. Simmer 3–5 minutes or until thickened. Add half-and-half and return to a simmer for 1 minute.

3. Add beans to pan and gently fold mixture all together until well coated. Place mixture in a 2–3 quart baking dish.

4. Bake 15 minutes and then sprinkle Crispy Shoestring Onions evenly over top and bake an additional 5–10 minutes until bubbly all over.

Italian Sausage Stuffing

Thanksgiving wouldn't be the same at Kate's house without her dad's famous stuffing! We use mild Italian sausage and then crank up the heat as desired with Tabasco sauce. If you already know you like it spicy, use spicy Italian sausage.

1 pound Italian sausage

1 medium onion, chopped

2 stalks celery, chopped

5–6 cloves garlic, minced

1 cup sliced mushrooms

1 grated Granny Smith apple (use your food processor if you have one; your knuckles will thank you)

1 (16-ounce) package stuffing or dressing mix (do not use seasoning packet)

2½ cups chicken broth

1 cup chopped pecans, toasted

½ plus cup dried cranberries, optional

1. Preheat oven to 350 degrees F. Spray a 9 x 13-inch baking dish with non-stick cooking spray and set aside.

2. Heat a very large skillet to medium heat, remove sausage casings, and crumble sausage into the pan. As it starts to brown, stir in onion, celery, and garlic. As the sausage cooks, break up larger pieces.

3. As the onion turns translucent, stir in mushrooms and apple.

4. When mushrooms are tender, sprinkle dressing mix over sausage mixture and add chicken broth. Continue stirring as dressing mix absorbs the liquid. Add pecans and cranberries, if desired. When the liquid has been incorporated and the mixture is fully combined, transfer to the prepared pan. Cover with aluminum foil and bake 10 minutes. Remove foil and bake another 10 minutes.

Serves 10–12

Make Ahead

ROLLOVERS
Celery
Mushrooms

TIP: To make this 1–2 days ahead of time, cover pan and refrigerate and then bake directly from the refrigerator.

❊ *Author's Note*

Even though my dad makes this recipe every year, he has never actually written down the recipe, so this is my interpretation of it. I do realize that I could get myself kicked out of the family for sharing secrets. — *Kate*

♥ **Family Favorite**

🌸 *Author's Note*

My college roommate used to make this all the time, and it was the ultimate comfort food during those first few years of college when I was trying to figure out how to be a grown-up. I've held onto it and tweaked it over the years, but it has a special place in my recipe collection as something that also taught me to love to cook. — *Kate*

Spanish Rice

This one-dish dinner is a family favorite comfort food at Kate's house. Savory, a tiny bit spicy, and loaded with vegetables, the leftovers might even be better than on the first night.

6–8 ounces bacon

1 medium onion, chopped

3–4 cloves garlic, minced

1 small (or ½ large) green bell pepper, seeded and chopped

1 (28-ounce) can stewed tomatoes, undrained

1½ cups water or chicken broth (2 cups for higher elevations)

2 tablespoons Worcestershire sauce

1¼ teaspoons kosher salt

1¼ teaspoons chili powder

⅛–¼ teaspoon Tabasco sauce, to taste

1¼ cups uncooked long-grain rice

1. Cook bacon until crisp, in a Dutch oven if possible. Remove from pan, crumble, and drain grease, reserving 2 tablespoons in the pan. Return the pan to medium heat and add onion, garlic, and bell pepper. Cook until onion is translucent.

2. While vegetables are cooking, pulse tomatoes 2–3 times in a blender to chop them. Pour into pan with vegetables. Add remaining ingredients and bring to a boil. Stir, cover, and reduce heat to low. Cook 20–25 minutes for low elevations or about 1 hour for high elevations or until rice is cooked, stirring occasionally to make sure rice is not burning.

3. When the rice is cooked, add the bacon and heat through.

⊕ **Quick and Easy**

🌿 **Vegetarian (see Tip)**

ROLLOVERS
Cream
Parmesan cheese
Parsley

TIP: For a vegetarian dish, substitute vegetable broth for the chicken broth.

Pear-Gorgonzola Farfalle

Sweet pears, robust Gorgonzola, and tangy cranberries are tossed with a creamy cheese sauce and bow tie pasta for a quick and elegant pasta dish.

8 ounces farfalle (bow tie) pasta (about 3 cups dry pasta)

3 medium pears, ripe but slightly firm

2 tablespoons butter

½ cup chicken broth

½ teaspoon kosher salt

⅛ teaspoon black pepper

6 tablespoons cream

1 teaspoon cornstarch

⅓ cup dried cranberries

½ cup crumbled Gorgonzola cheese

3 tablespoons chopped fresh parsley (or 1 teaspoon dried parsley)

¼ cup shredded Parmesan cheese, plus more for garnish

¼ cup chopped pecans, toasted, plus more for garnish

1. Cook pasta according to package instructions.

2. Peel and core pears and cut into ¼-inch slices. Cut slices in half horizontally.

3. Melt butter in a large skillet. Add pears and sauté on medium heat 1–2 minutes until slightly tender. Use a slotted spoon to remove pears from pan and set aside. Leave any remaining butter and pear juice in pan.

4. Add chicken broth, salt, and pepper to pan and bring to a simmer. Whisk cream and cornstarch together and add to pan. Return to simmer and cook 1–2 minutes, longer if needed, until slightly thickened. Add cranberries and simmer about 30 seconds. Remove from heat and immediately add Gorgonzola cheese, parsley, Parmesan cheese, and pasta. Toss to coat. Add pecans just before serving and top with additional cheeses and pecans, if desired.

Serves 10–12

☆ **Make Ahead**

🌿 **Vegetarian**

TIP 1: This dish can be prepped entirely 1 day ahead of time and stored in the refrigerator until ready to bake.

TIP 2: Sweet potatoes are easier to cut when cool, so consider baking and peeling them a day ahead of time. Store in refrigerator in a zip-top bag or sealed container until ready to use.

Baked Apples and Sweet Potatoes

Tender, flavorful sweet potatoes are baked with tart green apples and covered in a sweet, spiced sauce. All the wonderful flavors of fall meet in this side dish, perfect for a holiday table.

4 fresh sweet potatoes

4 tablespoons cornstarch

2 cups cold water

1 cup sugar

1 teaspoon salt

½ cup real butter, cut into small chunks

1½ teaspoons cinnamon

5–6 tart green apples, cored, peeled, and sliced into ¼-inch slices

2 cups miniature marshmallows, plus more if desired

1. Preheat oven to 400 degrees F. Line a baking sheet with aluminum foil and set aside.

2. Prick each sweet potato with a fork and place on prepared baking sheet. Place pan in oven and bake 45–60 minutes or until a knife can be easily inserted. Remove sweet potatoes and let rest until cool enough to handle. Remove skins (they should pull off easily) and slice potatoes into ¼–½-inch slices (see Tip 2). It's okay if they break into smaller pieces or chunks.

3. To prepare sauce, whisk together cornstarch and cold water in a small pan over medium heat. Add sugar, salt, and butter and stir until butter is melted and sauce is smooth. Remove from heat and whisk in cinnamon.

4. Place half of apple slices in an even layer on the bottom of a 9 x 13-inch pan lightly sprayed with cooking spray. Top with half of sweet potato slices. Drizzle half of sauce evenly over the top. Layer remaining apples and sweet potatoes and then drizzle with rest of sauce. Bake about 45 minutes at 350 degrees F. Sprinkle marshmallows on top and place under broiler until golden brown. Do not leave broiling marshmallows unattended unless you'd like the fire department invited to your Thanksgiving dinner.

Candied Coconut Sweet Potatoes

These sweet potatoes are pretty much going to be the star of your Thanksgiving dinner (or the midnight snack that follows). The crunchy praline topping alone will guarantee you rock-star status for years to come.

4 cups mashed sweet potatoes (about 4 medium sweet potatoes or 2 [28-ounce] cans)

6 tablespoons sugar

6 tablespoons real butter (no margarine), softened or melted

2 eggs, beaten

½ (14-ounce) can sweetened condensed milk

1 teaspoon vanilla

Topping

1 cup brown sugar

1½ cup sweetened coconut flakes

6 tablespoons melted butter

Serves 10–12

☆ **Make Ahead**

🥬 **Vegetarian**

TIP: This dish can be made completely 1 day ahead of time. Cover tightly with foil and refrigerate. Add 10–15 minutes to the baking time.

1. If using fresh sweet potatoes, preheat oven to 400 degrees F. Prick sweet potatoes with a fork and place them on a foil-lined baking sheet in the oven. Bake 45–60 minutes or until tender.

2. Once potatoes have cooled enough to handle, slice them in half lengthwise and scoop the insides into a mixing bowl.

3. Preheat oven to 350 degrees F.

4. Add sugar, butter, eggs, sweetened condensed milk, and vanilla to potatoes in the mixing bowl. Mix with an electric mixer until the desired consistency is reached. You can make it smooth or leave chunks of sweet potatoes in the mixture. Spread mixture evenly in a lightly greased 9 x 13-inch pan or in individual serving dishes, and set aside.

5. **For the topping:** Combine brown sugar and coconut and then add melted butter and mix gently. Sprinkle mixture evenly over sweet potatoes.

6. Bake 40–50 minutes, or less, depending on the size dish you use. The top should be browned and bubbly.

❦ Vegetarian (see Tip 2)

ROLLOVERS
Cream cheese
Parmesan cheese
Rosemary
Sage

TIP 1: Use a vegetable peeler to peel the squash and then cut it in half and use a spoon to scrape out seeds. Slice into long strips and dice into cubes. You can also look for diced butternut squash in the produce section of the grocery store.

TIP 2: For a vegetarian dish, omit the bacon and substitute vegetable broth for the chicken broth.

✳ Author's Note

This is a great way to sneak some vegetables into the family diet. The orange color from the pumpkin and squash mimics a cheese sauce, so kids (or picky spouses) have no idea they're eating their veggies.
Score: Mom–1, Picky Eaters–0.
—Sara

Roasted Butternut Squash Pasta with Pumpkin Sauce

Squash and pumpkin are perfect flavors to welcome in fall, but they can be a little overwhelming. These fall flavors are perfect here when combined with this creamy cheese sauce.

1 butternut squash, peeled and diced into ½-inch pieces (about 3 cups, see Tip 1)

1 medium yellow onion, diced into ½-inch pieces (about 1½ cups)

4 tablespoons chopped fresh sage leaves

1½ teaspoons minced fresh rosemary leaves

¾ teaspoon salt

¼ teaspoon black pepper

3 tablespoons olive oil

8 strips bacon

1 pound shell pasta

Pumpkin Sauce

1 cup low-fat milk

¾ cup chicken broth

2 ounces (¼ cup) cream cheese

2 tablespoons flour

¾ teaspoon salt

1 cup canned pumpkin puree

½ cup Parmesan cheese, additional for topping, if desired

1. Preheat oven to 425 degrees F. Line 2 large rimmed baking sheets with foil. Place squash, onion, sage, rosemary, salt, and pepper on one of the sheets. Drizzle with oil and toss gently with your hands until everything is well coated. Spread into a single layer.

2. If using bacon, lay it in a single layer on another baking sheet. Place both baking sheets in oven and cook 15–20 minutes or until bacon is crisp. Remove bacon pan from oven and use tongs to lay bacon strips on paper towels to drain. Crumble when cool enough to handle. Continue cooking squash an additional 13–15 minutes until it is soft and tender.

3. While the bacon and squash are in the oven, bring a large stockpot of water to boil and cook shell pasta according to package directions.

4. **For the sauce:** Combine milk, broth, cream cheese, flour, salt, and pumpkin puree in a blender and process until smooth. Pour mixture into a medium-sized saucepan and bring to a simmer. Simmer 4–5 minutes,

until thickened. Add Parmesan cheese, stir until melted, cover saucepan, and remove from heat.

5. Drain pasta and return to stockpot. Add sauce, squash mixture, and crumbled bacon and toss to combine. Serve immediately or transfer to a casserole dish, top with additional Parmesan cheese, and bake 15–20 minutes.

Halloween Party Food

You can throw an impressive Halloween party with some of these easy, kid-friendly ideas!

Mummy Dogs

This is a childhood favorite and one of the most popular of our Halloween spreads! Cut crescent roll dough into thin strips and wrap around hot dogs. Bake according to roll package directions and use ketchup or mustard for eyes. Cut hot dogs in half to make them bite-sized, if desired.

Monster Jaws

Quarter apples and take a wedge out of the center of each quarter. Dip apple pieces in water with a little lemon juice to prevent browning. Use toasted slivered almonds for teeth. Eyes are optional—you can stick pretzel rods in and attach candy eyes with peanut butter.

Dirt 'n' Worms (not pictured)

Another classic. Use chocolate pudding for the mud and put some crushed chocolate cookies on top for dirt. Hide gummy worms in the pudding for the eeek factor!

Breadstick Bones 'n' Blood

Use breadstick dough (store bought or homemade) and cut into strips. Use scissors to snip the ends into 2 pieces and roll them into bone shapes. Dip in "bloody" marinara! For extra flavor, sprinkle with garlic and Parmesan cheese.

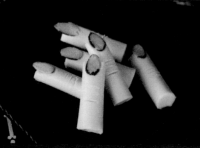

Cheesy Fingers

Super kid-friendly! Cut sticks of string cheese in half to make them kid-sized. Use the smooth edge of a knife to make knuckle marks and attach slivered almonds with a dab of cream cheese for nails. Use a knife to cut off just a bit of the cheese at an angle before attaching the almond.

Witch Hats

One of the easiest Halloween tricks (and treats!). Place a Hershey's Kiss on top of a Keebler Fudge Stripe cookie and you have a little hat. Using a little tube of frosting, which you can buy in the grocery store baking aisle, pipe a ring around the outside of the bottom of the kiss and press onto the cookie. It will squeeze out and make the ring around the kiss. Then pipe on the bow.

Spider Cookies

Red Hots and licorice turn chocolate sandwich cookies into creepy-cute spiders. Shoestring licorice is hard to find these days, but Twizzlers makes a pull-apart variety that works perfectly.

Pumpkin Sammies (not pictured)

This is a great staple for a Halloween party spread because it pleases both kids and adults and is something with substance! Use Halloween cookie cutters to cut your bread. Fill sandwiches with peanut butter or cream cheese and orange-colored jam (such as peach or apricot) for the kids and something more sophisticated, such as your favorite chicken salad, for the grown-ups!

Nutty Ghosts

Nutter Butters already look kind of like ghosts, making them perfect for this little treat! Give them a bath in some melted almond bark and put on a couple of mini chocolate chips for eyes.

Spider Web Dip

This trick works for pretty much any dip you can pipe sour cream on top of! A basic 7-layer taco dip is a great option. Put some sour cream in a plastic baggie, snip off a corner, and use it to draw a web pattern. Throw on a fake spider or two and your favorite party dip is instantly creepy!

Monster Munch: Sweet and Crunchy Autumn Snack Mix

This fun mix incorporates many of our favorite fall flavors. It's great for serving at parties, packaging up for friends and neighbors, or simply for snacking on!

12 cups popped plain or lightly salted popcorn

1 pound almond bark, melted according to package instructions

1 cup candy corn

1 cup dry roasted, salted peanuts

½ cup peanut butter candies, such as Reese's Pieces

Place popcorn in an extra-large mixing bowl. Pour melted almond bark over it and immediately add candy corn, peanuts, and Reese's Pieces. Using a wooden spoon or rubber spatula, stir mixture until everything is evenly coated. Spread mixture onto waxed paper or foil and let cool until almond bark hardens. Break up clumps and serve.

Apple Cider Floats

Serves 1

This single-serving treat is perfect for an afternoon when you've got a little time to yourself. However, it's easily modified to serve a crowd. Look for unfiltered apple cider for that fresh-from-the-orchard taste.

1 cup chilled apple cider

½ cup chilled ginger ale

1–2 scoops vanilla ice cream, or any seasonal flavor such as cinnamon or apple pie

Ground cinnamon and nutmeg, for garnish

1–2 tablespoons bottled caramel sauce

Pour apple cider and ginger ale into a glass. Add vanilla ice cream. Sprinkle on nutmeg and cinnamon, to taste, and drizzle caramel sauce on top. Serve immediately with a straw and a spoon.

Spiced Pumpkin Ice Cream Sandwiches

These ice cream sandwiches are perfect for the early fall when you're excited for autumn but it's still hot outside. You can also serve the ice cream at your Thanksgiving dinner with a slice of pie. For other seasons, you can always change the flavor of the cake mix and use your favorite homemade or store-bought ice cream to make ice cream sandwiches any time!

No-Cook Pumpkin Ice Cream

¾ cup brown sugar

1 teaspoon cinnamon

⅛ teaspoon ground ginger

⅛ teaspoon nutmeg

2 cups heavy cream

1 cup whole milk

1 cup canned pumpkin

2 teaspoons vanilla extract

Easy Spice Cookies

1 (18.25-ounce) spice cake mix

½ cup butter-flavored shortening

2 large eggs

Caramel sauce

1. **For the ice cream:** Make sure cream and milk are very cold. Whisk together brown sugar, cinnamon, ginger, and nutmeg in a mixing bowl. Add cream, milk, pumpkin, and vanilla. Whisk until brown sugar is dissolved. (You shouldn't feel any grains of sugar when you dip your finger in the mixture and rub your thumb against it.)

2. If you have time, refrigerate mixture for a few hours before putting into ice cream maker. If you're short on time, pour mixture directly into ice cream maker. Freeze according to manufacturer's instructions. When frozen, transfer ice cream to an airtight container and place in freezer to firm up—it should be scoopable but not frozen solid.

3. **For the cookies:** Preheat oven to 350 degrees F.

4. Combine cake mix, shortening, and eggs in the bowl of a heavy-duty mixer. The dough will be very stiff.

5. Using a cookie scoop, drop dough onto baking sheet. Use the bottom of a cup to lightly flatten the cookies. If dough sticks to the cup, spray cup

lightly with nonstick spray. Bake 5–7 minutes or until tops are cracked but cookies are slightly underdone. Allow to cool completely and then place in freezer to firm up.

6. **To assemble:** Spread your favorite caramel sauce onto flat side of a cookie. Add a small scoop of ice cream and then top with another cookie. Place on a waxed-paper-lined baking sheet in the freezer and repeat with remaining cookies.

7. When ready to serve, allow to stand at room temperature 5 minutes to soften slightly.

ROLLOVER
Cream

TIP: If using an actual pie, skip steps for apple pie filling and crust. Chop one-third to one-half of a baked apple pie into bite-sized pieces and add it to the custard when you're ready to freeze the ice cream.

Apple Pie Ice Cream

Leftover apple pie can be stirred into this creamy, cinnamon-y, custard-based ice cream. Or bake apples in butter and cinnamon and add them with chunks of cinnamon-kissed pie crust to the custard for a frozen treat that proves ice cream isn't just for summer. Top with a drizzle of your favorite caramel sauce.

Custard

1½ cups whole or 2% milk

1 cup sugar

2 eggs, separated

1 cup heavy cream

1 teaspoon cinnamon

1 teaspoon vanilla

Pie Crust (or use a refrigerated pie crust)

⅔ cup flour

Pinch of salt

6 tablespoons shortening

2–3 tablespoons ice water

½ tablespoon butter, melted

2 teaspoons sugar mixed with ⅛ teaspoon cinnamon

Apple Pie Filling (see Tip)

2 tablespoons softened butter, for rubbing pan

3 cups peeled, sliced Fuji apples (about 1½ pounds)

1½ teaspoons lemon or lime juice

¼ cup brown sugar

½ teaspoon pumpkin pie spice (or ¼ teaspoon cinnamon and ¼ teaspoon nutmeg)

1 tablespoon all-purpose flour

1. **For the custard:** Combine milk and sugar in a medium saucepan and heat over low until bubbles form around the edges. Whisk 2 egg yolks in a separate small bowl. Slowly add half of the heated milk mixture to egg yolks, whisking constantly. When mixture is fully combined, slowly pour mixture back into the saucepan with the rest of the milk, whisking constantly. Add cream. Insert a candy thermometer and cook on low until temperature reaches 160 degrees F., stirring frequently. Remove from heat and add cinnamon and vanilla. Allow to cool and then transfer to an airtight container and refrigerate. This step can be done 2–3 days before freezing.

2. **For the pie crust:** Combine flour and salt in a medium bowl and then cut in shortening with a pastry blender or two knives. Sprinkle in ice water, a little at a time, gently tossing dough until it forms a ball. Roll out crust onto a baking sheet and then brush with melted butter and

sprinkle with cinnamon sugar. Bake 12–14 minutes at 375 degrees F. or until golden brown. Cool completely. Gently break into chunks. You can also roll out a refrigerated pie crust instead of making your own.

3. **For the pie filling:** Preheat oven to 400 degrees F. Generously rub a 9-inch pie plate or a medium-sized, oven-safe skillet with butter. Peel apples and chop into bite-sized pieces. Toss with lemon or lime juice. Combine brown sugar, spices, and flour in a small bowl and sprinkle over apples. Toss apples in flour mixture and then place them in buttered pie plate. Cover with aluminum foil and bake 30–40 minutes or until apples are tender and syrupy. Allow to cool and then refrigerate until ready to use. This can be done 2–3 days before freezing the ice cream.

4. **For the ice cream:** When ready to freeze the ice cream, combine apples and custard. Pour mixture into ice cream maker and freeze according to manufacturer's instructions. When the machine is straining and ice cream is almost done, add baked pie crust pieces. Allow the machine to continue churning until pieces are incorporated. You can also mix in pieces by hand when ice cream is done churning.

5. Transfer ice cream to a freezer-safe container and freeze 3–4 hours or until it can be easily scooped. For best taste, freeze overnight. This will keep about a week in a freezer-safe container.

ROLLOVER
Cream

TIP 1: Candy thermometers may seem a little scary, but they can be helpful in both candy making and frying, and they only cost a few dollars.

TIP 2: Biting into these apples can be a pain, both literally and figuratively, so when the caramel and toppings have set up, use a sharp knife to cut the apples into slices.

VARIATION: If you want to make fancy dipped apples that you would spend a small fortune on at specialty candy shops, try out some of these toppings and mix and match to find your own favorites: Graham cracker crumbs; marshmallows; melted chocolate; melted peanut butter or white chocolate chips; chopped peanuts, almonds, pecans, or macadamia nuts; toasted coconut; crushed candy bars (Butterfingers or Heath Bars are great options); or dried fruits. Instead of rolling the apple in the toppings, try pressing a handful on with your hands to make sure it sticks to the caramel.

Honey Caramel Apples

Not only do these apples make gorgeous gifts for teachers and neighbors, they're a fun and delicious way to let your whole family participate in the fun! Coat these in caramel or mix and match toppings to make your own homemade gourmet caramel apples.

1 cup heavy cream

1 cup honey

Scant ¼ teaspoon salt

4 large (or 6 small) crisp apples, refrigerated for at least 1 hour

½ teaspoon vanilla extract

Desired toppings, optional (see Variation)

1. Combine cream, honey, and salt in a heavy saucepan over medium heat. Once warmed and whisked together, bring to a rolling boil. Reduce heat to simmer (it should still be bubbling, but not splattering over). Stir and scrape sides of pan down occasionally until a candy thermometer reaches 260 degrees F.

2. It may take about 30 minutes for the caramel to reach 260 degrees F., so while your caramel is cooking, prepare apples. Wash and dry them and then skewer them with a popsicle stick or bamboo skewer. Place in the refrigerator to continue chilling until ready to use.

3. Line a baking sheet or cutting board with waxed paper or parchment paper and set aside.

4. When caramel has reached 260 degrees F., remove from heat, add vanilla, and let sit 5 minutes, stirring occasionally. It should start to thicken. You'll have to eyeball the consistency for dipping. If you'd like to help it along, place your pan in a bowl of ice. If caramel gets too hard, return to heat until it's thin again.

5. Remove apples from refrigerator and dry them thoroughly with a towel. Dip in caramel, rolling and twirling each one until well coated. Let excess drip off and then place on prepared baking sheet. Refrigerate apples 10–20 minutes to set the caramel and then enjoy!

Peanut Butter Cup Cheesecake Tarts with Chocolate Mousse

This was our signature recipe from our last book launch, and we've kept it a big secret until now! Be sure to give these creamy individual cheesecakes plenty of time to chill before serving.

1 (12-ounce) bag mini peanut butter cups, divided

2 tablespoons creamy peanut butter

10 chocolate sandwich cookies, such as Oreos

1½ tablespoons butter, melted

1 (8-ounce) package cream cheese

¼ cup sugar

1 teaspoon vanilla

1 egg, room temperature

½ cup sour cream

Mousse Topping

1 teaspoon unflavored gelatin

2 teaspoons cold water

½ cup semisweet chocolate chips

1 cup heavy whipping cream, divided

1½ tablespoons sugar

1. Preheat oven to 375 degrees F.

2. Unwrap 16 mini peanut butter cups and place in a microwave-safe bowl. Add peanut butter and microwave at 30-second intervals, stirring in between, until melted and smooth. Set aside.

3. Process whole cookies in a food processor until they are crumbs. Add melted butter and mix to combine. Line a 12-cup muffin tin with foil liners. Drop about 1 tablespoon of crumb mixture into each foil liner and lightly press the crumbs down to form a crust.

4. Beat cream cheese and sugar until light and fluffy. Add vanilla and egg and beat on high 1–2 minutes. Turn speed down and, with the mixer running, add melted peanut butter cup mixture. Mix in sour cream and stir until combined. Divide batter evenly among the prepared foil liners, filling each one to within ¼-inch to ⅛-inch from the top. Bake about 15 minutes or until very light brown and still a little jiggly in the center. Remove from oven and allow to cool to room temperature. Refrigerate at least 4 hours or overnight.

5. **For the topping:** Place gelatin and cold water in a small bowl and set aside to soften. Place chocolate chips and 3 tablespoons cream in a

microwave-safe bowl and heat 30–40 seconds. Whisk until smooth, heating longer if necessary. Add softened gelatin and whisk to dissolve, making sure no lumps are left. Heat in microwave in 10-second intervals, if needed, to further dissolve gelatin. Allow to sit at room temperature about 10 minutes to cool until just warm. Place remaining cream in a medium-sized mixing bowl. Add the sugar and beat until medium peaks form. Add about one-fourth of the whipped cream to the chocolate mixture and stir. Gently fold in the remaining cream, one-fourth at a time, until incorporated. If the mixture is too soft to hold its shape, refrigerate 10 minutes. Otherwise, spoon on top of chilled cheesecakes and refrigerate at least 30 minutes to set up. Garnish with additional peanut butter cups.

Makes about 8–10 servings

♥ **Family Favorite**

VARIATION: For more chocolatey flavor in your popcorn, replace 1 cup peanut butter chips with 1 cup chocolate chips and then still drizzle the chocolate over the popcorn at the end.

Peanut Butter Cup Popcorn

This popcorn is perfect for fall football games and tailgating parties. Plus it combines three of our favorite things: peanut butter, chocolate, and popcorn!

2 bags of plain microwave popcorn (or about 16–18 cups of popped popcorn)

2 cups honey roasted peanuts

2 cups mini Reese's Peanut Butter Cups, roughly chopped, optional

3 cups peanut butter chips, roughly chopped

1 tablespoon vegetable shortening or oil

⅔ cup semisweet chocolate chips (see Variation)

1. Place popped popcorn, peanuts, and chopped peanut butter cups (if using) in a very large bowl. Combine peanut butter chips and vegetable oil or shortening in a microwave-safe bowl and heat 2–2½ minutes or until smooth, stirring every 30 seconds. Drizzle melted peanut butter chips over popcorn and peanuts and toss to combine.

2. Spread popcorn onto a waxed-paper-lined baking sheet. In a heavy-duty zip-top bag, heat semisweet chocolate chips until just melted and smooth (about 1–1½ minutes, mashing the bag every 20–30 seconds). Cut a small corner off the zip-top bag and drizzle chocolate over popcorn. Allow to stand long enough to become solid (you can transfer the pan to the refrigerator or freezer to hurry this step along). When chocolate is set up, break popcorn into small pieces and enjoy!

No-Bake Peanut Butter Cup Bars

With a cookie crust and a soft peanut butter filling, these chocolate-topped, no-bake treats taste just like one of our favorite candies . . .

Makes about 32 bars

♥ **Family Favorite**

25 chocolate sandwich cookies, such as Oreos

1 cup plus 4 tablespoons butter, divided

1½ cups plus 3 tablespoons creamy peanut butter, divided

1 pound (about 3½ cups) powdered sugar

1½ cups graham cracker crumbs

1 (12-ounce) bag semisweet chocolate chips

1. Line a 9 x 13-inch baking pan with foil that extends over edges of pan. Set aside.

2. Process whole cookies in food processor, or place in large zip-top bag and crush with a rolling pin until crushed into crumbs. Melt 4 tablespoons butter and stir into crumbs and mix until combined. Press crumbs evenly into bottom of the prepared pan and refrigerate while you prepare the next step.

3. Melt remaining 1 cup butter. Beat 1½ cups peanut butter, butter, and powdered sugar until combined. Add graham cracker crumbs and mix until incorporated. Press peanut butter dough evenly into pan on top of cookie crust.

4. Place chocolate chips and remaining 3 tablespoons peanut butter in a microwave-safe bowl. Heat in 30-second intervals, stirring in between, until melted and smooth. Pour chocolate mixture over peanut butter layer and spread evenly. Refrigerate bars about 2 hours. To serve, lift foil out of pan and use a large, sharp knife to cut into bars.

Cranberry Cinnamon Chip Bars

The aroma of cinnamon and cranberries in these easy bars will make your house smell like fall! Cinnamon chips are often a seasonal item found near the chocolate chips in the baking aisle of the grocery store.

½ cup real butter, melted

1½ cups graham cracker crumbs

1 (14-ounce) can sweetened condensed milk

1¼ cups shredded coconut

1 cup cinnamon chips

1 cup white chocolate chips

½ cup chopped pecans

½ cup dried cranberries

1. Preheat oven to 350 degrees F.

2. Pour butter into a 9 x 13-inch pan and spread with spatula to cover the entire bottom of pan. Sprinkle graham cracker crumbs over butter and spread evenly. Press down gently with fingertips. Pour sweetened condensed milk evenly over graham cracker crumbs. Sprinkle with coconut and continue layering with remaining ingredients: cinnamon chips, white chocolate chips, pecans, and cranberries, sprinkling each in an even layer. Press down gently with fingertips over entire pan.

3. Bake 25–30 minutes, until bubbly and slightly golden on top. Let cool completely before cutting.

Apple-Pear-Cranberry Crisp

This recipe combines some of our favorite fall flavors—apples, pears, cranberries, and cinnamon—baked together with a crunchy topping. Serve warm with vanilla ice cream or sweetened whipped cream.

Filling

5 cups peeled, sliced Granny Smith apples

5 cups peeled, sliced pears

1½ cups dried cranberries

¼ cup plus 2 tablespoons sugar

¼ cup packed brown sugar

2 tablespoons all-purpose flour

1 teaspoon ground cinnamon or pumpkin pie spice

Topping

1 cup oats

1 cup all-purpose flour

1 cup packed brown sugar

¼ teaspoon baking powder

¼ teaspoon baking soda

½ teaspoon cinnamon

1 cup chopped pecans, optional

½ cup butter, melted

1. Preheat oven to 350 degrees F.

2. **For the filling:** Combine apples, pears, and cranberries in a large bowl. Mix together sugars, flour, and cinnamon or pumpkin pie spice and sprinkle over fruit mixture. Toss mixture gently to coat fruit and then transfer to a 9 x 13-inch pan. Set aside.

3. **For the topping:** Combine oats, flour, brown sugar, baking powder, baking soda, cinnamon, chopped nuts (if using), and melted butter.

4. Crumble topping over fruit mixture and bake 45 minutes or until golden brown on top.

Author's Note

During the autumn months, I keep all of the ingredients for this recipe in my kitchen at all times. It's my go-to dessert for family get-togethers, or simply for casual dinners at home. —Sara

Pumpkin Crumble

This pumpkin crumble is a dressed-up version of pumpkin cobbler. Rich and creamy and loaded with fall spices and pecans, this is a perfect dessert for sharing with friends. Serve warm or at room temperature with a scoop of vanilla ice cream or sweetened whipped cream.

1 (18.25-ounce) white cake mix

¾ cup unsalted butter, room temperature, divided

1 (16-ounce) can pumpkin (about 1¾ cups pumpkin puree)

2 eggs

1 (14-ounce) can sweetened condensed milk

2 teaspoons cinnamon

½ teaspoon nutmeg

¼ teaspoon ground cloves

½ teaspoon ground ginger

⅛ teaspoon salt

¼ cup roughly chopped pecans

1. Preheat oven to 350 degrees F. Ignore directions on cake mix box and place mix in a medium mixing bowl and add ½ cup butter. Use your hands to combine mixture until it looks like dry crumbs.

2. Place half of mixture (about 1¾ cups) in an 8 x 8-inch pan and press into a flat, even layer. Reserve remaining crumbs for later.

3. Combine pumpkin, eggs, sweetened condensed milk, cinnamon, nutmeg, cloves, ginger, and salt in a separate bowl. Whisk until well combined. Pour pumpkin mixture over crumb layer in pan. Add pecans to reserved crumb mixture and then sprinkle on top. Melt remaining 4 tablespoons butter and drizzle over crumb topping.

4. Bake 35–45 minutes or until top is golden brown and a knife or skewer inserted in center comes out clean.

Glazed Maple Pecan Cookies

Sweet, buttery, and light, these melt-in-your-mouth cookies dipped in a maple syrup glaze are great for delivering to neighbors or snacking on while making Thanksgiving dinner.

1¾ cups all-purpose flour, lightly spooned into measuring cups and leveled with a knife

¼ cup cornstarch

1 cup butter, softened

½ cup brown sugar

¼ cup powdered sugar

1 egg yolk

1 teaspoon maple flavoring

1 cup finely chopped pecans, toasted (see Tip)

Glaze

1 tablespoon butter, melted

1 cup powdered sugar

1 tablespoon real maple syrup

1–2 tablespoons milk

Additional chopped or halved pecans for garnish, if desired

TIP: To toast pecans, preheat oven to 375 degrees F. Spread chopped pecans on a baking sheet in a single layer. Bake 5 minutes and then stir to redistribute nuts. Bake an additional 2–5 minutes, watching closely so nuts don't burn. Remove from oven when light parts of nuts are golden brown. Set aside to cool.

1. Preheat oven to 350 degrees F. Line baking sheets with parchment paper and set aside.

2. Whisk flour and cornstarch together and set aside.

3. Mix together butter and sugars at medium speed until creamy. Add egg yolk and maple flavoring, beating until well mixed. Reduce speed to low and gradually add flour and cornstarch mixture and toasted pecans. Measure dough by the scant tablespoonful and shape into balls. Place dough balls on baking sheets and press down lightly with fingers or the flat bottom of a drinking glass until dough is about ½-inch thick. Bake 9–12 minutes or until cookies puff and are very light golden brown.

4. **For the glaze:** Combine butter, powdered sugar, and maple syrup in a medium-sized mixing bowl. Add enough milk to make a glaze and whisk mixture until smooth.

5. When cookies have cooled, dip tops of cookies in the glaze and allow it to drip down the sides. Garnish with pecan halves or chopped pecans, if desired.

ROLLOVER
Cream

TIP: Since trifles can look messy when served out of a large bowl, try preparing individual servings in glasses or mini trifle dishes.

Gingerbread Pumpkin Trifle

This recipe takes cubes of classic gingerbread and layers them with a light and fluffy pumpkin mousse and sweetened whipped cream for an elegant and tasty dessert that will be a hit during the cold fall and winter months. To help make things even easier, make the gingerbread the day before and then cut it before preparing the trifle.

1 (14.5-ounce) box gingerbread mix

3 cups heavy cream

1 cup powdered sugar

1 teaspoon vanilla extract

Mousse

¼ cup cold water

1 (1-ounce) packet unflavored gelatin

1 (15-ounce) can pumpkin puree

½ cup brown sugar

1½ teaspoon cinnamon

⅛ teaspoon nutmeg, plus additional for garnish

⅛ teaspoon cloves

1. Bake gingerbread according to package directions in an 8 x 8-inch pan. Cool and cut into ½-inch cubes.

2. Combine heavy cream, powdered sugar, and vanilla in a large mixing bowl. Beat with electric mixer until medium-stiff peaks form and set aside.

3. **For the mousse:** Place water in a small, microwave-safe bowl and sprinkle gelatin over it. Gently stir and then set bowl aside for 5 minutes for gelatin to soften. Combine pumpkin, brown sugar, cinnamon, nutmeg, and cloves in a medium mixing bowl. Whisk to combine. Place bowl of gelatin in microwave and heat 30–40 seconds and then stir until dissolved completely. Add gelatin to pumpkin mixture and whisk until fully combined.

4. Fold one-third of whipped cream (about 2 cups) into pumpkin mixture, gently folding until incorporated.

5. Place half of gingerbread cubes on the bottom of a trifle bowl or other glass bowl with tall sides. Top with half of pumpkin mousse and half of remaining whipped cream. Repeat layers, ending with whipped cream, and sprinkle top lightly with nutmeg. Chill 1 hour before serving.

Thanksgiving Oreo Turkeys

Whether these are for eating or place-setting (or both!), these adorable, edible turkeys will get everyone at your Thanksgiving table in the mood for fun!

Double Stuf Oreo Cookies

Candy corn

Malt balls, such as Whoppers

Mini peanut butter cups, such as Reese's

Chocolate frosting spooned into an icing bag fitted with a Wilton size 2 or 3 tip

Yellow frosting*

Red frosting,* optional

Black sprinkles for eyes, optional

* For the little details, we like to use the small tubes of colored frosting found in the baking aisle (not the gel icing, which looks very similar). The chocolate frosting is easy to make. Homemade works a little better than store-bought frosting because you can make it stiffer with added powdered sugar.

1. Take a cookie and squeeze some chocolate frosting between the wafers over the top third or so (this is where the candy corn "feathers" will go).

2. Insert about 5 candy corns, tip-side down, into the crème filling where you have the chocolate frosting (Figure 1). Repeat with the remaining cookies.

3. Put a dab of chocolate frosting on the end of the cookie opposite the "feathers." Secure it to the base cookie, then place next to a wall while the frosting dries to keep the cookies in place (Figure 2).

4. Unwrap peanut butter cups. Using a sharp knife and a gentle sawing motion, cut a sliver off one side.

5. Flip cookies over, keeping them next to the wall if they need some extra support. Dab chocolate frosting onto a peanut butter cup and then place it on the cookie.

6. Using chocolate frosting, glue on a malt ball. Put frosting on the side of the malt ball that touches both the cookie and the peanut butter cup (Figure 3).

Figure 1

Figure 2

Figure 3

Figure 4

7. Using a dab of yellow frosting, glue on the white tip of a candy corn for a beak. Put two yellow dots on for eyes, and use a dab of chocolate frosting, a mini chocolate chip, or a little sprinkle for the black spots in the eyes (Figure 4). A sprinkle is really the perfect size.

8. Once beak is set in place, flip turkeys over and draw on little yellow feet. If you have red frosting (it usually comes in a set with the yellow), add a little wattle.

TIP: These make really cute place card holders for kids and adults! Just make little name cards and then stick them into the crème filling with toothpicks. It's a great way to get older kids involved.

White Chocolate Raspberry Cheesecake, see page 250

Winter

NEW YEAR'S

Christmas

VALENTINE'S DAY

WHAT WE LOVE

- peppermint and chocolate

- the silence of snowy nights

- the twinkle of Christmas lights

- pine needles and baking gingerbread

- sipping on hot chocolate with mini marshmallows after sledding

- reading books in front of the fire

- playing Secret Santa with favorite treats from the kitchen

- the season of Christlike giving and love

IN SEASON

Brussels sprouts, grapefruit, leeks, mushrooms, oranges, pears, sweet potatoes, tangerines, winter squash

WINTER

Hot Wassail

This festive hot drink can be served throughout fall and winter. It's also great for soothing sore throats year-round. Freeze leftovers in smaller portions to heat up when family members are feeling under the weather.

4 cups water

1 cup sugar

2 sticks cinnamon

¾ teaspoon ground cloves

3 cups pineapple juice

3 cups orange juice

3 cups lemonade

1. Combine water, sugar, cinnamon, and cloves. Simmer, covered, for 30 minutes and let sit 1 hour. This step can be done up to 3 days ahead of time.

2. Add pineapple juice, orange juice, and lemonade. Heat and serve.

Serves 12–14

☆ **Make Ahead**
🍲 **Slow Cooker**

SLOW-COOKER INSTRUCTIONS: Combine water, sugar, cinnamon, and cloves in the slow cooker. Cook on low all day. Add juices and lemonade and heat to serve.

TIP: For 1 serving, use ¼ cup cranberry juice, ¼ cup lemonade, and ½ cup ginger ale. Garnish with raspberries and lemon slices.

Sparkling Celebration Punch

This punch is a gorgeous, nonalcoholic way to ring in the new year!

4 cups chilled cranberry juice

4 cups chilled, fresh, homemade lemonade or high-quality, store-bought lemonade

1 (2-liter) bottle chilled ginger ale

1–2 cups fresh or frozen raspberries

2 lemons, sliced

Combine cranberry juice and lemonade in a punch bowl or large pitcher. Immediately before serving, pour the ginger ale over the lemonade mixture. Add raspberries and lemon slices and serve.

S'mores Hot Chocolate

Rich and decadent hot chocolate is everyone's favorite fireside treat in a mug, and this is great for serving to guests or while decorating the Christmas tree with your family.

2 tablespoons butter, melted	4 cups whole milk
2 graham crackers, crushed	8–12 large marshmallows
2 (4-ounce) milk chocolate bars	Chocolate syrup

1. Place melted butter in a small, shallow dish that is a little larger than the rim of your mug. Place crushed graham crackers in another dish of the same size. Flip mugs upside-down and dip the rims first in melted butter and then in the crushed graham crackers.

2. Break the chocolate into pieces and place one-half bar in each of the 4 mugs. Heat milk to a simmer and then carefully pour 1 cup into each mug over the chocolate. Set aside.

3. Place marshmallows on a parchment-lined baking sheet. Place under the broiler on low heat. Watch constantly and turn marshmallows after one side is toasted and browned. Broil until remaining side is toasted and then remove from oven.

4. Stir hot milk mixture to distribute melted chocolate. Top each mug with 2–3 toasted marshmallows and drizzle with chocolate syrup.

☆ **Make Ahead**
☺ **Quick and Easy**

ROLLOVERS
Bell pepper
Green onions

Cheese Ball

This cheese ball holds a special place in Kate's heart because it is solely responsible for getting her through the morning sickness of her second pregnancy. It's a festive classic for Christmas, but it's a great snack any time of year.

2 (8-ounce) packages cream cheese, softened (you can use light cream cheese)

2 cups (approximately 8 ounces) shredded sharp cheddar cheese

3 tablespoons finely chopped green onions

¼ cup finely chopped bell pepper, any color

1 teaspoon seasoning salt

1 (8-ounce) can crushed pineapple, drained very well (you may want to press in a fine-mesh strainer)

½ cup chopped pecans

1. Combine all ingredients except pecans. Add additional seasoning salt, to taste. Shape into a ball and refrigerate for several hours.

2. When ready to serve, remove from refrigerator and roll in chopped pecans. Serve with crackers and crunchy vegetables such as carrots, celery, and peppers.

Baked Brie

This indulgent, elegant holiday appetizer has creamy Brie slathered in sweet and spicy pepper jelly and baked in puff pastry. Spread it on crackers or fruit. Be sure to check out the variations, too!

½ package puff pastry, thawed for 40 minutes at room temperature

1 (8-ounce) wheel baby Brie

2–4 tablespoons pepper jelly

1 egg white mixed with a scant 2 teaspoons cold water

1. Preheat oven to 400 degrees F.

2. Gently unfold the puff pastry sheet, mending any tears in the pastry. Cut the Brie in half horizontally, making 2 circles. Place one half, rind down, on the pastry. Spread with jelly and then place the other half of the Brie, rind up, on the jelly. Fold pastry over the cheese, trimming excess pastry as needed, and then seal the edges. Cut decorative shapes from the excess dough. Place dough shapes on top and then brush entire top of pastry-cheese bundle with egg white and water mixture.

3. Place the cheese bundle, seam down, on a lightly greased baking dish. Bake 15–20 minutes or until the pastry is golden brown. Serve with crackers or bread, or with fresh strawberries, apples, pears, or grapes.

Serves 8–10

VARIATIONS:

Omit pepper jelly. Spread with one of the following:

- Chopped walnuts or pecans, honey, and a sprinkling of cinnamon
- Raspberry or strawberry preserves
- Dried cranberries or cherries

Makes about 3 dozen (2-inch) pieces

TIP: You can also cut the dough into pieces before placing them on the baking sheet—it's a little more work, but they're prettier that way.

Shortbread

Light, crisp, and buttery, shortbread disappears quickly, especially when it's coated in chocolate, toffee, or almond bark. Because there are so few ingredients, be sure they are the highest quality.

1 pound cold butter (no substitutions!)

1 cup packed brown sugar

4½ cups all-purpose flour (scooped lightly into measuring cups and leveled with a knife)

Chocolate chips, toffee, almond bark, or crushed candy canes, optional

1. Cut the cold butter into tablespoon-sized pieces and place them in the bowl of a stand mixer. Add brown sugar and beat with the paddle attachment until the mixture forms coarse crumbs, between the size of peas and marbles.

2. Add 3½ cups flour and mix until the flour is completely incorporated. Add the remaining 1 cup flour and mix 5 minutes. The dough should be soft and smooth.

3. On a parchment-lined baking sheet lightly sprinkled with flour, roll the dough into a rectangle and prick with a fork. Chill 30–60 minutes.

4. Preheat oven to 325 degrees F. Remove pan from refrigerator and trim the edges with a pizza cutter so the edges are smooth and even. Cut into squares, triangles, or rectangles (see Tip) and bake 20–30 minutes or until lightly golden on top. When the shortbread is cool enough to handle, separate into individual pieces.

5. It can be dipped in chocolate and topped with toffee pieces or spread with almond bark. To melt chocolate chips or almond bark, heat in a microwave in 30-second intervals until melted and smooth. Drizzle onto shortbread with a fork or place in a zip-top bag with a corner cut off. Sprinkle crushed toffee or peppermint candies while chocolate or almond bark is still wet and then let dry.

♥ Family Favorite

☺ Quick and Easy

ROLLOVER
Parmesan cheese

TIP 1: Look for tapioca flour or tapioca starch, as it's sometimes called, in the bulk foods or health foods section of a well-stocked grocery store, or in a health food store.

TIP 2: Try different kinds of cheese—we've used Monterey Jack, low-moisture mozzarella, Swiss, and Gruyère in place of cheddar, and they're all delicious!

❋ *Author's Note*

People with ties to Brazil surely have a place in their hearts for these little rolls called *pao de queijo*. It was one of the things I missed the most after serving as a missionary in Brazil and then coming back to the States. This method, taught to me by a local woman there, is about the quickest and easiest I've found, and the results are about the most authentic you can get! —*Sara*

Brazilian Cheese Rolls (Pao de Queijo)

These gluten-free, mini-popover-like rolls are one of Sara's favorite Brazilian recipes. They are light and fluffy and perfect to serve alongside a meal, or as a snack.

1 large egg

½ cup milk

¼ cup canola oil

1 cup tapioca flour (see Tip 1), no substitutions!

½ teaspoon kosher salt

¼ cup grated medium or sharp cheddar cheese (see Tip 2)

¼ cup grated Parmesan cheese

Extra cheese to sprinkle on top and any herbs or flavorings you'd like to add, optional. Rosemary and garlic powder are delicious!

1. Preheat oven to 400 degrees F. Lightly spray mini muffin pan with non-stick cooking spray. Set aside.

2. Place egg, milk, oil, tapioca flour, and salt in a blender and process until smooth. Add cheeses and pulse 2 times.

3. Immediately pour batter into a mini muffin pan, filling each well about ¾ full. We recommend sprinkling a bit of Parmesan cheese on top and/or a tiny sprinkle of kosher salt.

4. Bake 15–20 minutes until puffed and golden. Remove from oven and cool a few minutes before removing rolls from pan. Serve warm. These don't reheat well, so eat them immediately after baking them.

Baked Oatmeal

This cozy breakfast dish is kind of like a warm, soft oatmeal cookie doused in warm milk and eaten with a spoon. We love dried cranberries or dried cherries in this dish, but you can use any dried fruit you happen to have on hand.

3 cups rolled oats (not quick-cooking)

¾ cup brown sugar

2 teaspoons cinnamon

2 teaspoons baking powder

1 teaspoon kosher salt

¾ cup dried cranberries, raisins, dried cherries, or other dried fruit

1 cup milk

½ cup butter, melted (see Tip 1)

2 teaspoons vanilla extract

2 eggs

Optional toppings: chocolate chips, shredded coconut, toasted nuts, honey, almond or coconut milk

Serves 6–8

♥ **Family Favorite**

TIP 1: To cut down on the fat in this recipe, substitute ¼ cup applesauce for ¼ cup melted butter.

TIP 2: For a fun, family-style meal, set up an oatmeal bar with a variety of toppings and milks and let people customize their own bowls.

1. Preheat oven to 350 degrees F.

2. Combine oats, brown sugar, cinnamon, baking powder, salt, and dried fruit in a large bowl. Mix together milk, butter, vanilla, and eggs in a smaller bowl. Add the liquid mixture to the dry mixture and whisk to combine.

3. Pour into a deep 9-inch pie plate or an 8 × 8-inch or 9 × 9-inch baking dish, lightly sprayed with cooking spray. Bake 40 minutes or until the top is golden brown. Serve immediately with a splash of warmed milk and toppings, if desired.

❋ Author's Note

Growing up in Cache Valley, our family spent many, many Saturdays skiing at Beaver Mountain, and we always started our day with oatmeal raisin cookies for breakfast, which started a lifelong (and *completely* appropriate) association of cookies with breakfast. This oatmeal reminds me of those cold, snowy mornings. — Kate

Pear Pomegranate Salad

Sweet, juicy pears and tart pomegranate seeds are tossed with tangy feta cheese and a sweet red wine vinaigrette for a beautiful, festive salad that is perfect for the winter months. If you're having a hard time finding fresh pomegranates, you can substitute fresh raspberries.

½ cup chopped pecans

¼ cup sugar

1 head romaine lettuce

1 (14-ounce) bag baby spinach

Seeds from 1 pomegranate (about 1 cup)
  (see Tutorial, page 212)

2 ripe pears that are still a little firm

Juice of 1 lime

4 ounces crumbled feta cheese

1. Spray a sheet of aluminum foil with nonstick cooking spray and set aside.

2. Combine pecans and sugar in a small nonstick skillet. Cook over medium-low heat, stirring constantly, until the sugar melts and coats the nuts (about 15 minutes). Place on the prepared foil and set aside.

3. Toss together lettuce, spinach, pomegranate seeds, pears, lime juice, and cheese, adding the candied pecans right before serving. Drizzle Sweet Red Wine Vinaigrette over the salad and serve immediately.

Sweet Red Wine Vinaigrette

½ cup red wine vinegar

½ cup sugar

1–2 cloves garlic, roughly chopped

1 teaspoon kosher salt

1 teaspoon coarsely ground black pepper

½ cup canola oil

Combine vinegar, sugar, garlic, salt, and pepper in a blender and process on high. Lower speed, and while blender is running, add oil in a steady stream. Dressing may be stored in refrigerator about 2–3 weeks. Shake well before serving.

How to Cut and Eat a Pomegranate

Pomegranates are one of nature's super foods—delicious, and just plain gorgeous—but getting to the juicy seeds can be a little tricky if you've never done it before. Here are our step-by-step instructions, plus ideas on how to eat the seeds once you've gotten them out.

HOW TO PICK A RIPE POMEGRANATE: Unlike fruits such as bananas and mangoes that are picked while still unripe, pomegranates aren't picked until they're ripe and ready to eat, so technically if it's in the store, it should be ripe. That being said, sometimes you get ones that are better than others. Definitely feel for weight; a heavier fruit means more juice inside. Avoid any fruits that are shriveled, bruised, or have super soft spots.

1. Cut the top

Take a sharp knife (serrated works best) and slice off the top of the pomegranate just below the stem. Notice the distinct sections.

2. Score the skin

Using those segments as your guide, score the outer skin of the pomegranate from top to bottom. You don't want to cut all the way through the fruit, just the skin.

3. Break apart

Break the segments apart with your fingers. Since you didn't cut all the way through the fruit, all of the seeds should be intact, and it shouldn't be too messy. Aren't those gorgeous?

4. Remove the seeds

The fleshy seeds will easily come out with your fingers. Just bend back the skin and pull them out. You can also whack the hard skin with a wooden spoon, and the seeds will fall out easily as well.

We like to use the water method. Fill a medium-sized bowl with water and remove the seeds right over the bowl, or even under the water. The seeds will fall to the bottom and any white parts will float to the top. Any juice that comes out will go into the water and wash off.

5. Strain

Remove any white pith that is floating in the water and discard. Pour the remaining contents of the bowl into a strainer over the sink.

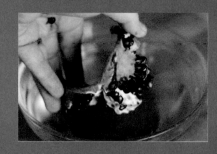

Give them a quick rinse with cold water, and they're all ready to eat!

We (and our kids) love eating the seeds straight from the bowl, but they're also delicious in salads, sprinkled on top of cereal or ice cream, or squeezed for their juice (although it takes about 2–3 pomegranates to yield 1 cup of juice).

FREEZER INSTRUCTIONS: Lay seeds in a single layer on a flat plate or baking sheet. Place in freezer 1–2 hours. When completely frozen, place in freezer-safe container or zip-top bag. Frozen seeds are especially great added to smoothies for an icy nutrient boost!

⊕ **Quick and Easy**

🌿 **Vegetarian**

ROLLOVERS
Red onion
Spinach

This recipe, which originated from my aunts, was one of the first "grown-up" salads I remember eating when I was young. I remember then, being captivated by the idea of juicy fruit, chewy raisins, and crunchy nuts in a side dish that I had previously known mostly for its iceberg lettuce and ranch dressing. It forever changed my salads!

—Sara

Spinach-Walnut Salad with Fresh Citrus

Crisp lettuce, tender spinach, toasted walnuts, and bright citrus all combine with a sweet and tangy dressing with flavors that are perfect for winter. Use golden raisins or dried cranberries instead of regular raisins, if you prefer.

1 head romaine lettuce, torn (about 6–8 cups)

3 cups loosely packed spinach

¼ cup thinly sliced red onion

⅓ cup raisins

½ cup roughly chopped walnuts, toasted

2 oranges, segmented (see Tutorial on page 216)

Dressing

⅓ cup white wine vinegar

¼ cup sugar

2 teaspoons Dijon mustard

3 tablespoons minced onion

1 teaspoon paprika

2½ teaspoons celery seed

1 teaspoon kosher salt

1 cup canola oil

1. Toss lettuce and spinach together in a large salad bowl. Sprinkle with onion, raisins, and walnuts. Top with dressing and toss to coat. Add orange segments and toss gently.

2. **For the dressing:** Combine vinegar, sugar, mustard, minced onion, paprika, celery seed, and salt in a blender and process until smooth, about 20–30 seconds. With the blender running on slow speed, add the oil in a slow, steady stream until incorporated. Pour the dressing into a jar or other container and refrigerate.

How to Segment Citrus Fruit

We love using citrus fruit in our recipes! Citrus is great in salads, but it's often avoided because no one wants the tough membrane on their fruit. This tutorial will teach you how to get around it so you can more easily use fresh oranges, grapefruits, nectarines, and other citrus treats. Segmenting is also a great way to introduce kids to eating citrus fruits without having to worry about choking hazards.

1. Cut off both the top and the bottom of the fruit so it sits flat.

2. Using a sharp knife and following the curvature of the fruit, cut the skin off in vertical cuts. Now you can see all of the natural segments. See those little white lines?

3. Insert your knife as close to that white line as you can get it and then do the same on the other side of the segment. Pull it right out! Continue until you have removed all of the segments.

4. The part that's left still has some juice in it, so squeeze it out and use it in a smoothie or a salad dressing, or simply drink it.

5. You're left with lovely little slices that you can use in your recipes.

Glass-Block Gelatin

This gelatin recipe is fun to make and eat and can be adapted to any holiday. If you never thought gelatin and "truly impressive" could ever be used in the same sentence, seeing the looks on people's faces when you serve this might change your mind . . .

Serves 14–16

♥ Family Favorite

7 cups water plus a little extra, divided

4–5 (4-serving size) gelatin packages, such as Jell-O, in assorted colors

2 packets unflavored gelatin

1 (14-ounce) can sweetened condensed milk

1. Spray nonstick cooking spray inside 1 small, square food storage container for each color gelatin you are going to use. Set aside.

2. Bring 5+ cups of water to a boil. Combine 1 cup boiling water with 1 package of gelatin, stirring until dissolved. Transfer the dissolved gelatin to one of the prepared containers. Repeat with the remaining packages of gelatin. Refrigerate for at least 4 hours, but preferably overnight.

3. When the gelatin has set, bring another 1½ cups of water to a boil. While the water is heating, sprinkle 2 packets of unflavored gelatin over ½ cup of cold water. Allow to stand about 4 minutes. Pour the boiling water over the dissolved gelatin and stir to combine. Add the sweetened condensed milk and mix well. Allow to cool to room temperature.

4. Lightly spray a 9 × 13-inch pan with nonstick cooking spray. Carefully cut the colored gelatin into ½-inch cubes and gently toss to combine in the pan. Pour the cooled milk mixture over the colored gelatin and, if necessary, rearrange some of the colored gelatin to make sure it is evenly distributed and not sticking out of the milk mixture too far.

5. Place pan in refrigerator and chill overnight. Cut into squares, rectangles, or various shapes with cookie cutters and serve.

♥ **Family Favorite**
☺ **Quick and Easy**

ROLLOVERS
Basil
Cream

Easy Creamy Tomato-Basil Soup

If canned tomato soup has lost its appeal for you, try this super-easy, grown-up version of the childhood classic. Serve with grilled cheese sandwiches or your favorite panini.

1–2 tablespoons extra virgin olive oil

5–6 cloves garlic, minced or pressed

1 small onion, chopped

2 (15-ounce) cans fire-roasted diced tomatoes

4 cups (2 cans) chicken or vegetable broth

¾ cup vegetable juice, such as V8

3 tablespoons chopped fresh basil

¼ cup plus 2 tablespoons heavy cream (add more, if desired)

Cooked pasta (such as orzo or broken spaghetti) or 1 (8–10-ounce) package cheese tortellini, optional

Cooked, crumbled ground beef, ground turkey, or Italian sausage, optional

Salt and pepper, to taste

1. Heat oil in a large stockpot over medium heat. Add garlic and onion and sauté for about 5 minutes or until garlic is fragrant and onion is translucent. Add undrained tomatoes, broth, and vegetable juice. Bring to a boil, reduce heat, and simmer about 10 minutes.

2. Add the basil and remove from heat. Using an immersion blender, blend the mixture until the desired consistency is reached. If you don't have an immersion blender, the soup can be processed in batches in a standard blender. Add cream and any optional ingredients you desire—such as meat and pasta—and stir to combine. Season to taste with salt and pepper.

Potato-Leek Soup with Ham

This creamy, comforting soup flavored with smoky ham, mellow leeks, and herbs and spices is great for a chilly winter afternoon. Leeks have a mild onion flavor and pair beautifully with creamy Yukon Gold potatoes.

Serves 6–8

ROLLOVERS
Cream
Parsley

4–5 medium leeks

3 tablespoons butter

3 cloves garlic, minced

1 teaspoon kosher salt

¼ teaspoon black pepper

1½ pounds Yukon gold potatoes (about 2–3 medium), diced into ½-inch cubes

4 cups chicken broth

2 bay leaves

1 teaspoon dried thyme

8 ounces ham, diced (about 2 cups)

¾ cup cream

1–2 tablespoons minced fresh parsley

1. Slice ends off leeks just above the root and discard. Cut leeks in half lengthwise. Starting at the white end, slice the leeks crosswise (as you would slice a green onion) in ¼-inch slices. Stop slicing when the leaves turn from pale green to dark green and discard the remaining part of the leek. Place sliced leeks (about 2 cups) in a bowl of cold water and stir with fingers to loosen layers and remove any dirt. Drain and set aside.

2. Melt butter in a large stockpot over medium heat. Add leeks, garlic, salt, and pepper and cook about 3–5 minutes, stirring often, until leeks are wilted and fragrant. Add potatoes, broth, bay leaves, and thyme. Bring to a simmer and cover pot. Simmer on medium-low heat about 15 minutes or until potatoes are fork-tender. Mash slightly with the back of a spoon to break them up. Add ham and simmer 5 more minutes. Add cream, parsley, and additional salt and pepper, to taste. Heat until warmed through. Remove bay leaves and serve.

Vegetable Beef Barley Soup

Serves 10–12

♥ Family Favorite
❋ Freezer Meal
☆ Make Ahead

TIP: Because this soup serves so many, consider serving part of it immediately and then freezing the rest for later. When ready to serve, place the block of frozen soup in a slow cooker and cook it on low all day, or defrost on half power in microwave until thawed and then on full power until heated through.

This hearty, healthy soup is loaded with whole grains, lean meats, and vegetables and is great for feeding a crowd. It's good the first day, but it's really delicious the second day, so you might want to consider making it a day in advance and then heating it up right before serving.

1 pound lean ground beef

1 medium onion, minced

1 envelope dry onion soup mix

1 (28-ounce) can diced tomatoes, undrained

1 (12-ounce) can vegetable juice, such as V8

2 cups water

3 cups beef broth

4 carrots, peeled and chopped

6 ounces cut green beans (fresh or frozen)

1 tablespoon dried parsley

⅛–¼ teaspoon red pepper flakes

1 bay leaf

Salt and pepper, to taste

½ cup barley or quinoa

1. In a large stockpot, cook the ground beef and onion until the ground beef is cooked and onion is tender and translucent. Add the soup mix and stir until beef is completely coated in the mix.

2. Add the remaining ingredients, except the barley or quinoa. Bring to a boil, cover, and then simmer 1–2 hours. Add salt and pepper, to taste.

3. About 30 minutes before the soup is done, cook the barley or quinoa according to package directions and add to the soup. Remove bay leaf before serving.

Beef Enchiladas with Red Sauce

Using corn tortillas in these enchiladas helps make them a little bit different—kind of like tamales without all the work! If you prefer lots of sauce with your enchiladas, use 2 cans of enchilada sauce before popping the pan into the oven.

1–2 tablespoons extra virgin olive oil

1 pound lean ground beef

1 medium onion, minced

3 cloves garlic, pressed

1 green pepper, finely chopped

1 tablespoon chili powder

½ teaspoon cumin

½ teaspoon coriander

½ teaspoon oregano

½ teaspoon freshly ground black pepper

¾ teaspoon kosher salt

1 cup sour cream, plus more for garnish, if desired

Juice of 1 lime

1 cup shredded pepper Jack cheese

2 tablespoons chopped fresh parsley or cilantro, plus more for garnish

1 (8-ounce) can tomato sauce

10–12 small flour or corn tortillas

1–2 (10-ounce) cans of your favorite red enchilada sauce

2 cups shredded cheddar or Colby Jack cheese

1. Preheat oven to 350 degrees F.

2. Heat oil in a large skillet over medium heat. Add ground beef, onion, garlic, green pepper, chili powder, cumin, coriander, oregano, black pepper, and salt and cook until onion is translucent and the meat is fully cooked. Remove from heat.

3. Stir in sour cream, lime juice, pepper Jack cheese, parsley or cilantro, and tomato sauce. Place ¼ cup filling on each tortilla, roll up, and place in pan. Top with enchilada sauce and then cheddar or Colby Jack cheese. Bake uncovered 20–25 minutes, or until cheese is melted and bubbly. Serve with a dollop of sour cream and chopped parsley or cilantro, if desired.

Serves 6–8

♥ Family Favorite
☆ Make Ahead

ROLLOVERS
Cilantro
Parsley
Sour cream

TIP: To help prevent tortillas from cracking, wrap a few tortillas at a time in damp paper towels and microwave 20–30 seconds or until heated through.

MAKE-AHEAD INSTRUCTIONS: These can be made 2–3 days ahead of time and stored in the refrigerator, tightly covered. Add the enchilada sauce and cheese right before placing in the oven.

🍲 **Slow Cooker**

TIP: Pepperoncinis and banana peppers can vary widely depending on your region. We've found Vlasic banana peppers to be consistently mild while Marzetti pepperoncinis can be quite spicy, so keep that in mind when you're at the grocery store.

Pepperoncini Beef Sandwiches

If you love Our Best Bites *Slow Cooker French Dip Sandwiches, think of these as the just-as-attractive younger brother. Which sandwich we like better is definitely a toss-up!*

2 tablespoons olive or cooking oil

½ teaspoon kosher salt, plus more if needed

½ teaspoon freshly ground black pepper, plus more if needed

3 pounds beef roast, trimmed of excess fat

4–5 cloves garlic, minced or pressed

1 (16-ounce) jar sliced pepperoncinis or banana peppers, undrained (see Tip)

Crusty sandwich rolls

Mayonnaise (light mayonnaise is fine)

Sliced provolone cheese

1. Heat oil in a pot or high-sided skillet over high heat. Combine salt and pepper and rub it into the meat. Add more salt and pepper, if desired.

2. When the oil is hot, sear the roast on all sides so the outside is browned and a little crispy. Transfer the roast to a slow cooker and add garlic and pepperoncinis.

3. If possible, cook on high until the liquid comes to a boil and then turn to low and cook until the roast shreds easily with a fork, for a total cooking time of about 6–8 hours. Or cook on low 8–10 hours until the beef is fork-tender.

4. For sandwiches, slice the rolls and spread lightly with mayonnaise; top with shredded beef. Add a slice of provolone cheese and then place under the broiler 1–3 minutes or until the bread is toasted and the cheese is melted. Serve immediately.

ROLLOVER
Rosemary

TIP 1: When estimating serving sizes, remember that each rib will serve about 2 people.

TIP 2: Slice refrigerated leftover roast in very thin slices and place on buttered and toasted rolls. Top with provolone or Swiss cheese and broil to melt. Serve with instant au jus for French dip sandwiches that will knock your socks off.

Author's Note

In my home growing up, beef ruled the holiday table. My dad was always in charge of that part of the meal, and prime cuts of meat always involved lots of garlic. He taught me all his tricks for cooking perfect, tender, flavorful roasts—including his signature method of inserting fresh garlic cloves right into the meat. Now beef rules most of my holiday tables as well! —Sara

Garlic-Rosemary Rib Roast

Prime cuts of beef can be intimidating to cook because of their high price tag. Follow these instructions for a flavorful roast that will be worth every penny. It's sure to be the hit of any holiday table.

1 (7–8-pound) rib roast (about 4 ribs)	1 tablespoon kosher salt
¼ cup olive oil	1½ teaspoons pepper
¼ cup minced fresh rosemary	3–4 additional garlic cloves, sliced in half lengthwise, optional
¼ cup minced garlic	

1. Let roast stand 20–30 minutes at room temperature.

2. Preheat oven to 475 degrees F. Trim excess fat, but leave a thin layer on top of roast. While roast is resting, combine oil, rosemary, garlic, salt, and pepper.

3. Place roast bone side down in large roasting pan.

4. Optional step: Take a thin, sharp knife and poke directly into roast vertically, cutting about three-fourths of the way down. Make several incisions, about 2 inches apart around the top of the roast. Take the optional garlic cloves and place a half into each incision, using a finger or a knife to push it into the center of roast. Gently press openings shut with fingers when finished.

5. Pour rosemary mixture over top of roast and use your hands to massage the mixture onto all sides of roast, except the bottom.

6. Place roast in oven, uncovered, for 20 minutes. Without opening oven door, reduce heat to 350 degrees F. Continue cooking 2–3 hours until roast reaches an internal temperature of 135 degrees F. for medium rare, and 145–150 degrees F. for medium. Keep in mind that the temperature will continue to rise a few degrees after roast is removed from oven. Do not cook past 150 degrees F. or meat will be overdone. For best results, use an oven-safe thermometer that stays in the roast for the whole cooking process so you can take it out at the right time.

7. Remove pan from oven, cover loosely with foil, and let rest 15 minutes.

8. For easy carving, first remove the rib bones. Run a sharp knife between

top of ribs and roast to remove ribs completely. Slice roast and serve immediately.

9. If the roast yields significant amounts of pan juices, skim off fat and serve drippings with meat. If the roast lacks juices, serve the roast alone, or whip up a quick gravy with thickened beef stock or store-bought au jus.

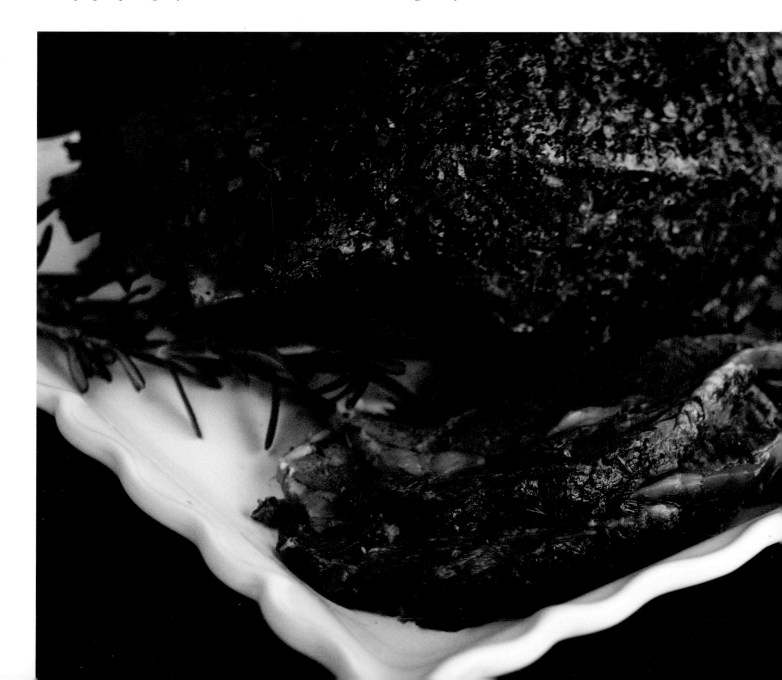

ROLLOVERS
Green onions
Parsley

TIP: Because this particular cut of beef is so lean, the bacon helps keep the steaks moist and flavorful. It can be removed before serving, or left on. If you have a kitchen torch, crisp the bacon before serving.

Garlic Herb Butter

½ cup real butter, softened

¾ teaspoon pressed or finely minced garlic

1½ tablespoons finely minced green onion

1 tablespoon minced fresh parsley

2–3 cracks freshly ground black pepper

Combine butter, garlic, green onion, parsley, and pepper with a fork and stir until well incorporated. Place butter on a rectangular sheet of plastic wrap. Wrap plastic around the butter and gently roll to create an even round log shape. Twist ends of plastic wrap to secure. Place in refrigerator to chill until ready to use. It can be prepared ahead of time and refrigerated.

Pan-Seared Filet Mignon with Garlic Herb Butter

This elegant, indulgent dish is perfect for Valentine's Day. Spread some of the leftover garlic herb butter on warmed French bread or toss with halved, boiled red potatoes. For a classic steakhouse meal, pair this dish with mashed potatoes and a homemade Caesar salad (page 82, without the chicken).

Up to 4 (6–7-ounce) fillets	Freshly cracked black pepper
1 slice bacon for each fillet (not thick cut)	1 tablespoon olive oil
Kosher or sea salt	1 tablespoon butter

1. Remove fillets from refrigerator and let them rest 20–30 minutes at room temperature.

2. Preheat oven to 400 degrees F. Rinse steaks in cool water and blot dry with paper towels. Wrap a piece of bacon around each steak, trimming if necessary so the ends don't overlap much, and secure with a toothpick or tie with baker's twine. Sprinkle each side of steak generously with salt and pepper.

3. Heat an 8–10-inch, oven-safe skillet to medium-high heat on the stove top. Use a stainless steel skillet if you have one. Add oil and butter and tilt pan until butter is melted. Place steaks in pan and cook, without moving them, about 2½ minutes. Use tongs to gently turn steaks and cook on remaining side for 2½ minutes. Place skillet in oven and cook until internal temperature reaches 130–135 degrees F., about 5–8 minutes. Leave an oven-safe thermometer in the meat so you can remove the steaks at just the right time. This particular cut will taste best when cooked medium rare. The quickest way to ruin this prime cut of beef is to overcook it!

4. Remove steaks from oven and top with a slice of Garlic Herb Butter. Let steaks rest about 3 minutes as butter melts. Serve immediately with more butter, if desired.

♥ **Family Favorite**
❄ **Freezer Meal**
☆ **Make Ahead**

ROLLOVERS
Mushrooms
Parmesan cheese

TIP: One 12-ounce box of pasta shells will have more shells than needed. We like to cook the entire package anyway, to account for any broken shells after cooking. If you have unused cooked shells, consider cutting them into smaller pieces and tossing them into a soup later in the week.

MAKE-AHEAD

INSTRUCTIONS: To prepare ahead of time, cover pan tightly in plastic and then in foil. Refrigerate 1–2 days and then bake as directed (making sure to remove plastic layer underneath foil), or freeze up to two months. Thaw frozen dish in refrigerator overnight and then bake as directed, or bake from frozen, covered in foil (remove plastic wrap), about two hours or until heated and bubbly throughout. Cooking times vary from frozen so check periodically during cooking.

Stuffed Shells with Sausage and Mushrooms

These rich and cheesy stuffed shells are lightened up with turkey sausage. Serve with a loaf of garlic bread and a tossed green salad.

1 (12-ounce) box jumbo pasta shells

1½ tablespoons butter

8 ounces cremini mushrooms, stems discarded and caps diced

1 (15-ounce) container ricotta cheese

2 eggs, lightly beaten

1 teaspoon garlic powder

½ teaspoon onion powder

¾ teaspoon dried oregano leaves

2 teaspoons dried basil leaves

¼ teaspoon kosher salt

¼ teaspoon freshly cracked black pepper

12 ounces Italian turkey sausage (sweet or hot, depending on your preference)

1 (9-ounce) box frozen spinach, thawed, or 6 cups loosely packed fresh spinach

2½ cups shredded mozzarella cheese, divided

1½ cups shredded Parmesan cheese, divided

1 (26-32 ounce) jar marinara sauce

1. Preheat oven to 350 degrees F.

2. Cook pasta shells al dente according to package instructions.

3. Heat a medium skillet to medium heat. Melt butter and add mushrooms. Sauté 3–4 minutes until mushrooms are golden brown. Place ricotta in large mixing bowl. Add eggs, garlic powder, onion powder, oregano, basil, salt, and pepper. Stir to combine. When mushrooms are cooked, add to ricotta mixture and return empty skillet to stove top.

4. Squeeze sausage out of casings and add to skillet. Break up with a spatula and cook until browned and crumbly. Add sausage to ricotta mixture.

5. If using thawed spinach, squeeze moisture from spinach and roughly chop. If using fresh spinach, roughly chop. Add spinach to ricotta-meat mixture and fold together. Add 2 cups mozzarella and 1 cup Parmesan to mixture.

6. Spread marinara sauce evenly on bottom of a 9 x 13-inch pan. Fill each pasta shell with 2 rounded tablespoons of filling and nestle snugly in the pan on top of the sauce. You should be able to fill and fit in about 24–26 shells. Top with remaining ½ cup mozzarella and ½ cup Parmesan cheeses. Cover with foil and bake 50–60 minutes or until bubbly all over. Remove foil about 10–15 minutes before end of baking time.

Roasted Red Potatoes with Pearl Onions

Roasted red potatoes feel like the perfect winter food and, when tossed with pearl onions, herbs, and butter, they're a great side dish made with produce that's easy to find in the winter.

2 tablespoons butter

1½ tablespoons extra virgin olive oil

4–5 cloves garlic, minced

¾ teaspoon kosher salt

¼ teaspoon black pepper

¼ teaspoon dried dill weed, plus addtional for garnish

1½ pounds baby red potatoes (1–2 inches in diameter, or larger potatoes halved or quartered to size)

1 (4-ounce) bag frozen pearl onions, thawed

Juice of 1 medium lemon (about 2 tablespoons)

1. Preheat oven to 400 degrees F.

2. Place butter, oil, and garlic in a small, microwave-safe bowl. Heat until butter is melted, about 20–30 seconds. Add salt, pepper, and dill weed. Stir and set aside.

3. Place potatoes and onions in a 9 x 13-inch baking dish. Drizzle with butter mixture, scraping sides of bowl, and toss to coat evenly. Bake 30 minutes and then gently stir potatoes and onions. Cook 20–30 minutes more, until potatoes are tender and onions are soft and starting to caramelize. Remove pan from oven and squeeze fresh lemon juice over potatoes. Toss and sprinkle with a little extra dill, if desired.

Oven-Roasted Balsamic Brussels Sprouts

Serves 4–6

⏱ **Quick and Easy**

Brussels sprouts are kind of a love-em-or-hate-em veggie, but roasting these little guys helps bring out their natural sweetness. Look for very young sprouts or, if you can find them, sprouts that are still on the stalk—they'll be sweeter and won't have the sulfur odor.

1 pound fresh Brussels sprouts

1½ tablespoons extra virgin olive oil

2½ tablespoons balsamic vinegar, divided

3–4 cloves fresh garlic, minced

½ teaspoon kosher salt, plus more to taste

¼ teaspoon freshly ground black pepper

1. Preheat oven to 425 degrees F. Line a baking sheet with aluminum foil and set aside.

2. Rinse sprouts in cool water and then cut off the tough ends. Pull any scraggly leaves off the sprouts and then cut each sprout in half. Place in a medium-sized bowl.

3. Whisk together oil, 1½ tablespoons balsamic vinegar, garlic, salt, and pepper in a small bowl. Drizzle over the sprouts and then toss to combine. Spread the sprouts evenly on the baking sheet and roast 20–25 minutes or until crisp-tender.

4. Remove from oven and transfer to a serving dish. Drizzle with 1 tablespoon vinegar and sprinkle with kosher salt, to taste. Serve immediately.

Makes 16–18 (2-inch) pops or 6 (4-inch) mini pies

Sweetie Pie Pops

These tiny, adorable pie pops are the perfect size for slipping into a packed lunch and are a sweet way to say "Happy Valentine's Day!"

Apple Pie Filling*

1 medium tart green apple, peeled and shredded

¼ teaspoon ground cinnamon

1 tablespoon packed brown sugar

1 tablespoon flour

1½ teaspoons lemon juice

1 tablespoon cold butter, shredded

Canned pie filling may also be used.

Pie Pops

1 unbaked pie crust (homemade or store-bought)

6-inch lollipop sticks (available at craft stores)

Small bowl of water

2 tablespoons butter, melted

Coarse sugar or sprinkles for topping

Glaze

½ cup powdered sugar

1 tablespoon butter, melted

1–3 teaspoons milk

1. **For the pie filling:** Combine all ingredients.

2. Preheat oven to 375 degrees F. Line a baking sheet with parchment paper or a silicone baking mat, if desired.

3. **For the pie pops:** Roll out pie crust dough on a floured surface about ⅛-inch thick. Cut out heart shapes (or other shapes of your choosing) and place them on your baking sheet.

4. Place about 1–2 teaspoons of filling on each dough cutout, keeping filling at least ¼ inch away from the edges.

5. Place a 6-inch lollipop stick in center of shape, with the top of the stick near the top of the shape. Wet your finger in a small bowl of water and wet the edge of the pie crust shape. Wet the edges of a second pie crust shape (one without filling) and place on top of the other. Press together gently with your fingers to seal the cutouts together.

6. Use a fork to crimp edges, being sure to seal edges around the stick. Poke a fork once into top of pie so steam can vent. If desired, brush top of pie with melted butter and sprinkle with sugar (or leave plain to glaze after baking).

7. Bake pies 15–20 minutes or until barely golden brown. Cool for a few minutes and then transfer to a cooling rack.

8. **For the glaze:** Whisk together all ingredients until smooth. Add milk until desired consistency is reached. Gently brush or spoon glaze over pies while still warm. Cool completely before packaging. If desired, place in cellophane bags and tie with ribbons and labels.

Peppermint-Kissed Chocolate Cookies

Kate whipped these cookies together on a whim a few years ago, using Sara's Cadbury Egg cookie dough recipe. We never imagined they would be the hit they have become! Topped with a striped peppermint kiss, these cookies are as delicious as they are adorable.

½ cup real butter, softened

½ cup butter-flavored shortening

1 cup brown sugar

1 cup sugar

2 eggs

1½ teaspoons vanilla extract

1 teaspoon peppermint extract, optional, but recommended

1 teaspoon baking powder

1 teaspoon baking soda

½ teaspoon salt

2½ cups flour, lightly spooned into measuring cups and leveled with a knife

¼ cup plus 2 tablespoons unsweetened cocoa powder

1 (12-ounce) bag dark or semisweet chocolate chips

48 Hershey's Candy Cane Kisses, unwrapped (one [10-ounce] bag)

1. Preheat oven to 350 degrees F.

2. Cream together softened butter, shortening, and sugars 1–2 minutes on medium-high speed or until light and fluffy. Add eggs, vanilla, and peppermint, if using. Combine baking powder, baking soda, salt, flour, and cocoa powder in a separate medium-sized bowl. Add to butter-sugar mixture and mix until combined. Mix in the chocolate chips.

3. To prevent cookies from flattening, refrigerate dough 30–60 minutes. Drop dough by the tablespoonful onto an ungreased baking sheet. Bake until just set but centers are still soft, about 8 minutes. Remove from oven and allow to cool 1–2 minutes. Use a metal spatula to transfer cookies to cooling rack. Top each cookie with an unwrapped Candy Cane Kiss. Allow cookies to cool completely, long enough for the candy to harden. If necessary, after the cookies have cooled, they can be placed in the refrigerator or freezer to re-solidify the candy kiss.

Makes 12 large or 16 medium
squares

♥ **Family Favorite**
☆ **Make Ahead**

ROLLOVER
Cream

CUPCAKE VARIATION:
Bake 1–2 tablespoons brownie batter
in cupcake liners. Once cooled and
chilled, layer remaining ingredients on
top as noted in recipe. Pipe on whipped
topping (color with food coloring first, if
desired) and freeze until firm.

Mint-Chip Brownie Ice Cream Squares

This family favorite is great to serve a crowd. It can be made ahead of time and stored for several days in the freezer if wrapped well. Try switching up the flavors for other holidays and events and watch it disappear like magic!

1 (19–23-ounce) box brownie mix

1 (1½-quart) mint chocolate chip ice cream

1 cup dark or semisweet chocolate chips

½ cup cream

½ teaspoon peppermint extract

15–20 Oreo cookies, crushed

1 (8-ounce) container whipped topping

Green food coloring, optional

Shaved or curled chocolate or sprinkles, optional

1. Line a 9 × 13-inch pan with foil and let foil extend at least 1 inch over edges of pan. Bake brownies according to package instructions. Cool completely and place in freezer to chill.

2. Soften ice cream, either by letting it sit at room temperature and stirring every 10 minutes, or by heating at half power in the microwave until you can stir it easily with a spoon. It should be the consistency of frosting. Gently spread evenly over brownies. Place pan in freezer to chill while you prepare the next step.

3. Place chocolate chips in a bowl. Heat cream in microwave until hot and bubbly. Pour cream over chocolate and cover bowl with plastic wrap. Let sit 5 minutes and then whisk until smooth. Whisk in peppermint extract and let chocolate mixture cool almost to room temperature. Drizzle evenly over ice cream in pan. Sprinkle crushed cookies evenly over chocolate and lightly press in with your hands. Spread whipped topping in an even layer over all. If desired, sprinkle shaved or curled chocolate, or sprinkles on top.

4. Freeze at least several hours (and up to several days, covered), until firm. When ready to serve, let sit at room temperature about 10–15 minutes to soften. Remove entire dessert from pan by picking up foil edges. Cut into squares and serve.

This is my family's most beloved Christmas cookie. My mom has been making them since I was a little girl, and friends and family eagerly await the gift plates each year. It's never officially Christmas until I eat one of these cookies. When I was young, my job was to press the fingerprint into the dough, and now my own kids help with that step!—*Sara*

Candy Cane Cookies with Chocolate Mint

A unique rolling technique gives these cookies a sugar-crusted outer layer with a soft, buttery center. The candy-cane-studded dough and cool, chocolate-covered mint on top makes them irresistible! These cookies improve after sitting overnight, so feel free to make them ahead if you want to.

¾ cup real butter, room temperature

½ cup sugar, divided

1 egg, separated

1 teaspoon pure vanilla extract

2 cups flour, lightly spooned into measuring cup and leveled with a knife

½ cup crushed peppermint candy canes

Junior Mint candies (about 40, or 2 [1.84-ounce] boxes)

1. Preheat oven to 350 degrees F.

2. Cream butter and ¼ cup sugar until light and fluffy. Stir in egg yolk and vanilla. Add flour gradually, ¼ cup at a time, and beat until fully incorporated. Stir in candy canes and mix just until combined and well distributed.

3. Beat egg white with fork until frothy, about 30 seconds. Place remaining ¼ cup sugar in a shallow bowl. Roll dough into balls about ¾ inch in diameter. Dip balls in egg white, letting excess drip off so only a light coating remains and then roll in sugar. Use additional sugar, as needed. Place balls on a parchment-lined baking sheet about 2 inches apart. Lightly press finger in center of dough to make indentation. Bake 8–10 minutes, or until just puffed in the centers and set on the outside edge. Remove pan from oven and very quickly place a Junior Mint candy in the center of each cookie. Return pan to oven for one minute. Remove and let cool for 2 minutes.

4. Transfer cookies to cooling rack and let cool completely before eating. Store in an airtight container between layers of parchment or waxed paper for up to 3 days. Recipe doubles well.

Peppermint Fudge Cupcake Jars

Chocolate Cupcakes (page 53)

Frosting Recipe (page 58)

8 (8-ounce) wide-mouth Mason jars (the short, squatty kind)

1. Prepare Chocolate Cupcake batter.

2. Place the Mason jars on a cookie sheet. Divide the cupcake batter evenly among the 8 ungreased jars. Fill about half full or a little less. Bake until a toothpick inserted into the center of a jar comes out with only a few moist crumbs attached, about 22–25 minutes. Remove from oven and carefully (with a pot holder!) transfer jars to a cooling rack. Let jars cool to room temperature before topping with Peppermint Ganache.

3. To assemble, pour 1½–2 tablespoons ganache over the top of each cupcake jar. If desired, use a paring knife to first hollow out a well in the middle of the cake. Tilt jars to distribute ganache evenly over the top of the cupcakes and then let cool for the ganache to set. If storing overnight, place lids and rings on jars and leave at room temperature.

4. Make your favorite frosting. Add peppermint extract (in addition to the vanilla extract) by ¼ teaspoon, to taste (we prefer at least ½ teaspoon). Follow the Striped Frosting tutorial at right to create a red-and-white striped look, or the Swirled Multicolored Frosting technique on page 60 with pink and white frostings. Pipe frosting into each jar, leaving room for the lid. If desired, sprinkle with crushed candy canes before putting lids on jars.

Peppermint Ganache

4 ounces semisweet chocolate (chocolate chips are fine)

½ cup heavy cream

¼ teaspoon peppermint extract or ⅛ teaspoon peppermint oil

Place chocolate chips in a bowl. Heat cream in microwave until bubbles form around the edge. Pour over chocolate chips and immediately cover bowl with plastic wrap. Let sit 5 minutes, add peppermint extract, and then whisk until smooth. Cool uncovered until thickened slightly, almost like a thin pudding.

Striped Frosting Instructions

To make red-and-white-striped frosting, prepare a frosting bag fitted with a piping tip of your choice. Fold top edge of bag over to expose the inside of bag. Use a small, clean paint brush dipped in gel-style food coloring and "paint" stripes directly onto your piping bag, starting from the tip and extending 3–4 inches up the sides of the bag. (See photo at right.) Carefully spoon white frosting into the bag and use as usual.

STORAGE: If completed through the ganache step (before frosting), screw lids on and refrigerate for 3–4 days and then frost right before gifting. If you plan to completely prepare them a day or two ahead, we recommend *reversing* the filling and topping. Cut out the center of the cupcakes and fill with frosting. Place the "cap" of the cupcake back over the hole and then cover the entire top with ganache and a sprinkling of candy cane. Store at room temperature for 1–2 days or refrigerated for 3–4 days.

Crafty in the Kitchen

Candy Penguin Cupcakes

These adorable penguins might look too cute to eat, but we made sure that every part of the penguin was delicious so that when the time came, you'd enjoy every bite of it.

TIP: These adorable cupcakes are a lot of work, but if you're patient and careful, they're really pretty easy. It's also easy to divide up the steps—make the cupcakes one day, do the bodies of the penguins another, and finish them on a third day. If you do it all at once, it takes about 3–4 hours from the time you begin baking the cupcakes until the penguins are finished.

Unfrosted cupcakes, any flavor

White frosting (Choose your favorite, see page 58)

1 (12-ounce) bag semisweet chocolate chips

2 tablespoons shortening

1 (10-ounce) bag large marshmallows

Sanding sugar, white sparkly sugar, or white sprinkles

Candy corn

Coconut

Trolli Gummi Strawberry Puffs or large gumdrops

1 cube almond bark

Yellow or orange Starbursts

SUPPLIES
Bamboo skewers

Block of craft foam

1 pair kitchen shears

1 large zip-top bag

2 small zip-top bags (snack size is perfect)

Figure 1

Figure 2

1. Make the cupcakes and the white frosting, but do not frost the cupcakes yet.

2. Combine chocolate chips and shortening in a microwave-safe bowl. Heat in microwave, stirring about every 30 seconds, until chocolate is completely melted and flows easily.

3. While chocolate is melting, insert a bamboo skewer about halfway into the flat end of each marshmallow. Stick the other end into craft foam.

4. Working quickly in batches of six at a time, dip each skewered marshmallow into the chocolate and tap the skewer against the edge of the bowl a few times to remove excess chocolate. Reinsert the skewers with the dipped marshmallows into the craft foam so the chocolate can harden without touching anything (Figure 1).

5. When you've dipped about 6 marshmallows, wash your hands to remove any trace of chocolate. Pour a small amount of sanding sugar, sparkly sugar, or sprinkles onto a plate. Using your kitchen shears, carefully cut a thin slice (about ⅛-inch thick) of plain marshmallow. Dip the sticky side (or just one side if both sides are sticky) into the sanding sugar (Figure 2). Carefully place the non-sugared side onto a dipped marshmallow. The melted chocolate will hold the marshmallow slice in place. Repeat with remaining dipped marshmallows.

6. Next, take two candy corns and place them directly above (they'll end up on the bottom, though) the penguin's tummy with the fat, yellow end poking out (these are his feet). Form a little V-shape with the white ends so the feet stick out at an angle. This is a great stopping point if you need several days to complete the project (Figure 3).

Figure 3

7. When chocolate is firm and you're ready to continue working, frost your cupcakes. The easiest and fastest way is to fill a large zip-top bag with frosting, cut ½ inch off a corner, and then squeeze the frosting onto the cupcakes. After you've squeezed all the frosting from the bag, spread it across the tops of the cupcakes with a butter knife (Figure 4).

8. Place a penguin on each frosted cupcake and gently press some coconut around each penguin body (for snow). Use more sanding sugar or white sprinkles instead of coconut, if you prefer.

Figure 4

9. Remelt the chocolate and give it a good stir. Dip each Trolli strawberry candy into the chocolate and then twirl it a little to remove the excess chocolate. Carefully place the dipped candy onto the penguin's body, the oblong side directly above the penguin's tummy (this will be his face). (Figure 5.)

10. Wash your hands again and then open the yellow or orange Starbursts. A little Starburst will go a long way here; in fact, we used only two Starbursts for 24 cupcakes, so keep that in mind. Carefully cut off a small piece of the Starburst (maybe a ⅛-inch corner) and then form it into a beak between your fingers. Carefully place it in the middle of the penguin's face (the chocolate on the head will still have to be warm for this to work).

Figure 5

11. Place the cube of almond bark into a small zip-top bag and seal it. Heat in the microwave about 1 minute, checking it every 20–30 seconds (mash it around with your hands a little each time), until the bark has melted.

12. While almond bark is melting, scrape the excess dipping chocolate into the other small zip-top bag. Reheat if necessary.

13. At this point, place the cupcake on a box on your work station so that you can rest your elbows on the work station while you finish the eyes. Cut a *tiny* hole in the corner of each bag and then carefully dot each penguin head with two dots of melted almond bark.

14. As the final step, take the zip-top bag of melted chocolate and make an even tinier dot on the white almond bark for the irises. This is when their little personalities come out.

Cinnamon Chocolate Cookie Bark

This festive candy will melt the hearts of those you love! Break into chunks and package up for gifts, or make it just for munching!

½ cup red hot candies

10 chocolate sandwich cookies, such as Oreos

1 pound almond bark

¼–½ teaspoon cinnamon-flavored oil

2 tablespoons semisweet or dark chocolate chips

Red and/or pink candy melts and assorted pink and white candies such as M&M's and cinnamon bears, optional

1. Line a large, rimmed baking sheet with parchment paper or a silicone baking mat and set aside.

2. Place red hots in a heavy-duty zip-top bag and smash with a meat mallet or hammer to crush. Alternately, you could pulse them in a food processor a few times until they are roughly chopped. Break up cookies into rough chunks, either by hand, in a zip-top bag, or in a food processor. Following package instructions, melt almond bark until smooth in a medium-sized, microwave-safe bowl. Add cinnamon oil to taste and then gently stir in red hots and chocolate cookies.

3. Pour mixture onto prepared baking sheet and gently spread it into an even layer about ¼-inch thick. If desired, sprinkle on additional candies. If using cinnamon bears, you may want to slice them so they are thinner. Melt chocolate chips in microwave in 30-second intervals until smooth. Drizzle over almond bark mixture. If desired, melt colored candy melts and drizzle those over as well.

4. Let mixture harden completely and then break into chunks. Can be stored in an airtight container for several days.

Makes 1 pound of bark

TIP: Almond bark is a candy coating similar in taste and texture to white chocolate. It contains no nuts or nut products. You can find it in the baking aisle of the grocery store, often in holiday displays during peak holiday seasons.

VARIATION: Turn this bark into a festive popcorn mix by pouring the melted cinnamon almond bark mixture over 16 cups air-popped or lightly salted popcorn. Stir to evenly coat, let dry, and break into pieces. Drizzle with melted semisweet chocolate, if desired.

Peppermint Mousse Cake

Chocolate and peppermint are two of our favorite flavors, and they combine here in this stunning, peppermint mousse-filled cake, perfect for a festive end to Christmas dinner.

Cake

1 (18.25-ounce) box devil's food cake mix (we prefer Duncan Hines)

10 round peppermint candies or 2 candy canes, crushed

Chocolate-Peppermint Ganache

6 ounces semisweet or dark chocolate chips (about 1 cup)

¾ cup heavy cream

¼ teaspoon peppermint extract

White Chocolate Mousse

1 teaspoon unflavored gelatin

2 teaspoons cold water

½ cup white chocolate chips

1 cup heavy cream, divided

1 tablespoon sugar

1 teaspoon peppermint extract

Red food coloring

1. **For the cake:** Prepare cake mix according to package directions and bake in two 8- or 9-inch round pans. When baked, remove from oven and cool on a rack 15 minutes. Use a knife to make sure cake is separated from pan edge and then invert to remove from baking pans. Place on cooling rack until completely cooled. Cakes may be made several days in advance and stored in the freezer if well wrapped.

2. **For the ganache:** Place chocolate chips in a medium bowl. Set aside. Microwave cream 1–2 minutes, until hot, and then pour over chocolate chips. Allow to stand 5 minutes, add peppermint extract, and then whisk until smooth. Set the ganache aside to cool and thicken.

3. **For the mousse:** Place gelatin in a small dish and add cold water to soften it. Set aside. Place white chocolate and 3 tablespoons cream in a microwave-safe bowl. Heat in 30-second intervals, stirring after each interval, until the mixture is melted and smooth. Add the softened gelatin to the white chocolate mixture and stir with a whisk until smooth. Transfer the mixture to a large bowl to cool until just barely warm, about 10–15 minutes. If the mixture starts to solidify, microwave in 10-second intervals until smooth again.

4. Whip remaining cream, sugar, peppermint extract, and a few drops of red food coloring in a separate bowl until medium peaks form. Stir one-fourth of the whipped cream into the white chocolate mixture to lighten it. Then gently fold in remaining cream, a little at a time. Refrigerate mousse about 15 minutes until slightly set.

5. **To assemble:** Use a large knife to cut rounded tops off cake layers. Place one layer on a serving plate. Spoon mousse on top and spread out to edges. Place second layer on top of mousse. Refrigerate cake about 30 minutes. When the chocolate ganache has cooled and thickened slightly, slowly spoon it on top of the cake. If it has thickened too much, warm it in the microwave for a few seconds at a time. Starting in the center, slowly spread it on cake in a circular motion. Keep spooning and spreading the ganache until some drips over the edges. Sprinkle crushed candy canes on top. Refrigerate the cake until 30 minutes before serving.

Peppermint Ice Cream with Chocolate Sauce

This unique recipe doesn't require an ice cream machine! Cool peppermint and dreamy chocolate combine for one decadent dessert, and not even Santa Claus needs to know how easy it was to make.

2 cups whipping cream (not heavy whipping cream), divided

1 (14-ounce) can sweetened condensed milk, divided

2½ tablespoons butter

¾ cup semisweet or bittersweet chocolate chips

1 teaspoon vanilla extract

1 teaspoon peppermint extract

½ cup crushed candy canes (4–5 medium candy canes)

1. Place ½ cup cream and 5 tablespoons sweetened condensed milk in a small saucepan. Add butter and chocolate chips. Heat on medium-low heat, stirring frequently until melted and smooth. Cool sauce to room temperature and place in an airtight container in refrigerator until ready to serve.

2. While sauce is warming, place remaining sweetened condensed milk in a large mixing bowl and stir in vanilla and peppermint extracts.

3. In a separate mixing bowl, whip remaining 1½ cups cream until medium-stiff peaks form. Fold whipped cream into sweetened condensed milk mixture in 3 additions (see Tip for how to fold in mixtures), gently folding until combined. Fold in crushed candy canes. Place mixture in an airtight, freezer-safe container and freeze for at least 6–8 hours, until firm, preferably overnight.

4. When ready to serve, heat sauce in microwave for 30 seconds, stir, and heat again if needed until warm. Serve over ice cream.

5. To omit the fudge sauce from this recipe, do not use butter or chocolate chips. Simply use the entire 2 cups cream and entire can sweetened condensed milk in the recipe and continue as recipe instructs

🌸 *Author's Note*

I love making cheesecakes for special celebrations because I'm forced to plan ahead and have it all done the day before! It allows more time for enjoying the special day and also for getting the kitchen cleaned before we dig into dessert. This particular cheesecake has an amazing flavor combination that tastes especially decadent. —*Sara*

White Chocolate Raspberry Cheesecake

Sweet and decadent, this is the perfect finale for any Valentine's Day dinner.

Raspberry Sauce

12 ounces frozen unsweetened raspberries (about 3 cups)

½ cup sugar

3 tablespoons water, divided

1 tablespoon cornstarch

Crust

2½ cups chocolate sandwich cookie crumbs (about 25 cookies, such as Oreos)

6 tablespoons butter, melted

Cheesecake

1 cup white chocolate chips

3 (8-ounce) packages cream cheese, softened

1 cup sugar

3 large eggs, at room temperature

1 teaspoon almond extract

1 teaspoon vanilla extract

2 tablespoons flour

¾ cup sour cream

Fresh raspberries, for garnish

White chocolate curls, for garnish

1. **For the sauce:** Place frozen berries, sugar, and 2 tablespoons water in a medium saucepan on medium heat. Stir occasionally, mashing berries with your spoon, until the mixture comes to a boil. Reduce heat to simmer and cook 5 minutes. Combine remaining 1 tablespoon water with cornstarch in a small bowl and then add mixture to sauce. Stirring constantly, allow to simmer 1–2 minutes until slightly thickened. Pour sauce through a fine-mesh strainer to remove seeds. Set aside. This sauce can be made several days ahead of time and stored in the refrigerator.

2. **For the crust:** Combine the cookie crumbs and melted butter. Press the mixture onto the bottom and 1 inch up the sides of a 10-inch springform pan.

3. Preheat oven to 350 degrees F.

4. **For the cheesecake:** Place the white chocolate chips in a microwave-safe bowl and heat in 30-second intervals, stirring after each, until the chocolate is melted and smooth.

5. Beat cream cheese and sugar in a separate mixing bowl until smooth. Add eggs one at a time, beating after each addition. Add extracts, flour,

and sour cream and beat just until combined. With the mixer running, add the melted white chocolate in a steady stream and mix just until incorporated.

6. Pour half the cream cheese mixture over the cookie crust and spread evenly. Drizzle 2 tablespoons raspberry sauce over the top and use a knife to swirl the sauce into the filling. Pour remaining filling on top and drizzle another 2 tablespoons raspberry sauce over the top. Use a knife to swirl the sauce.

7. Place the springform pan on top of 2 layers of heavy-duty foil. Wrap the foil up the sides of the pan to prevent water from leaking into the pan. Place the foil-wrapped pan into a larger shallow pan, such as a large roasting pan, and place in the oven. Pour enough hot water into the larger pan to reach about two-thirds up the sides of the cheesecake pan. Bake 70–80 minutes or until the cheesecake is set on top and very lightly golden around the edges. Cheesecake should have a slight jiggle when gently shaken.

8. Remove both pans from the oven and let cheesecake sit in the water bath for 30 minutes. Remove the springform pan from the water and remove the foil. Place the pan on a cooling rack until cooled to room temperature. Cover and refrigerate for 6–8 hours.

9. When ready to serve, gently remove the sides from the springform pan and cut cake into 10–12 slices. Serve with remaining raspberry sauce drizzled on top and garnish with fresh berries and white chocolate curls, if desired.

Peppermint Bark Popcorn

One of the most popular holiday recipes on our blog, this unique treat is great for sharing with friends, neighbors, and coworkers or for having on hand at home when you're getting ready for Christmas!

12–14 cups popped popcorn (freshly popped, or about 2 bags microwave popcorn, see Tip 1)

1 pound almond bark (found in the baking aisle of the grocery store)

½ teaspoon peppermint oil or 2 teaspoons peppermint extract (see Tip 2)

1 (6-ounce) box candy canes, crushed (about 1 generous cup; we love Bob's brand!)

¾ cup semisweet or dark chocolate chips

1. Place popcorn in a very large mixing bowl.

2. Melt almond bark according to package instructions. When completely melted, add extract or peppermint oil. If using extract, it's normal for the almond bark to seize (get lumpy), which is okay. Just stir very quickly—the more you wait, the more it will seize.

3. Pour melted almond bark mixture over popcorn and pour crushed candy canes on top. Stir to coat popcorn evenly. Spread the popcorn out onto waxed paper, parchment paper, or foil.

4. Place chocolate chips in a microwave-safe bowl and heat in 30-second intervals, stirring in between, until melted and smooth. Use a fork to drizzle over popcorn mixture. Let mixture cool completely so chocolate and almond bark are hardened. You may refrigerate to speed process along.

5. When chocolate is hardened, use your hands to break up popcorn into chunks. Put in a bowl, a jar, a cute box, or in your mouth.

Rollover Ingredients

We've created this index to help you plan meals and use up perishable or uncommon ingredients.

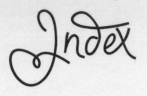

Index

About the Authors

Sara Smith Wells was born and raised in the Seattle area. Inspired by the lush green surroundings of the Pacific Northwest, she earned a degree in horticulture from Brigham Young University and put her talents to work as a landscape designer. Her knack for design, as well as a lifetime passion for culinary exploration and entertaining on the spur-of-the-moment, resulted in catering opportunities, which allowed Sara to showcase her belief that food can taste great and be beautiful as well. She has since become an avid photographer and enjoyed styling and photographing the recipes in this book.

Sara served an LDS mission in Curitiba, Brazil, where she picked up a love of fresh ingredients and a taste for Latin flavor that influences much of her cooking today. She and her husband, Eric, currently reside in Boise, Idaho, where they cook, eat, laugh, and play with their three young sons, Tyler, Owen, and Jack.

Kate Randle Jones was born and raised in Logan, Utah, where she dabbled in cooking, but never seriously. After her sophomore year at Brigham Young University, she married Sam Jones, and they suddenly found themselves to be the stereotypical broke college student couple. Due to the fact that they needed to eat and she needed a hobby, Kate began cooking and baking nearly everything from scratch. Once she got comfortable in the kitchen, she started experimenting with different tastes, recipes, and methods.

She graduated from BYU in 2004 with a degree in English and considers herself beyond lucky that she gets to do her two favorite things: write and cook. In her spare time, she loves to read, entertain, and travel (or, at the very least, think about traveling!). She currently lives in an old house with a big yard in Louisiana with her husband, Sam, and her three children.